# Thriving As
# An Empath

# Thriving As An Empath

## EMPOWERING YOUR HIGHLY SENSITIVE SELF

**Trevor N. Lewis**
**Abbigayle McKinney**

ISBN: 153317797X
ISBN 13: 9781533177971

# Contents

# Preface

We expect the reader will notice our very different writing styles.

Trevor is an English baby boomer with a British, stiff upper lip, and Abbey is a generation Y, informal, salt-of the-earth Southern gal born in America. Each has encouraged the other to move closer to middle ground while retaining their natural characters.

We hope you enjoy the blend!

# CHAPTER 1

# Introduction

By Trevor

> *And therefore as a stranger give it welcome. There*
> *are more things in heaven and earth, Horatio,*
> *than are dreamt of in your philosophy.*
> —WILLIAM SHAKESPEARE (HAMLET, ACT 1, SCENE 5)

## Why This Book Is for You or Someone You Love

- Were you described as an over-sensitive child?
- Do you pick up energy from other people?
- Do you feel worse when you are around crowds?
- Do you find it hard to watch the news or sad/violent movies?
- Do you sense when someone is not telling the truth?
- Do you have mood swings for reasons that you often don't understand and can't control?
- Do you have other experiences that modern science can't explain (such as telepathy, knowing future events, or knowing current events happening far away)?

If you or someone you love can answer yes to most of those questions, then this book is for you! It will help you understand these traits and most importantly, be able to work with them. Instead of thinking of them as liabilities or even curses, they will become a useful part of your everyday life.

## What Is in This Book?

This book describes both what the term *empath* means and what it does not mean. It covers a host of different tools, techniques, and coping mechanisms, to move you forward from being a confused empath to being a thriving empath. Different people will resonate with different exercises, and we do not intend for you to use all of them, only for you to know what processes are available.

As empaths, most of us put other people first. Then, only once we've taken care of everybody else, do we take care of ourselves. Unfortunately, this only works as a very short-term strategy. There is a reason that on an airplane, we are told to put on our own oxygen mask before taking care of the person next to us. We need to be healthy, centered, and have a good understanding of what it means to be an empath if we are to best help those around us. Because of this, the second half of the book puts an emphasis on self-care and discusses things like physical exercise, diet, meditation, and breath work.

You will see three individual chapters on shielding, grounding, and releasing. The chapters on self-care tools, crystals, and herbs also include aspects of all three. It is not about favoring any single one of them. Sometimes the emphasis may need to be on shielding, other times on grounding or releasing, but all three have a role to play in being a balanced, thriving empath.

Of course, any one of these topics could be volumes on their own. We are not trying to cover these topics in depth but only to touch on them from the empath's perspective. This book is intended primarily to be a guide for beginner empaths, although many established empaths may well find many new ideas here. Instead of presenting extensive detail, we want to pique the reader's interest by including references for further reading. Especially in such mainstream areas as diet and exercise, we have aimed these reference points somewhat off the beaten track. See what catches your interest; try the processes, see what works, and then reach out to other books and Internet searches based on the ideas we have shared here.

## Mental Health

This book is not intended to offer mental health counseling. Many individuals with the characteristics common among empaths do experience mental health challenges. Empaths process other people's emotions while often thinking that those emotions are their own; this fact is a challenge in itself. Being an empath in a mainstream world that has no idea where to begin understanding us is perhaps an even greater challenge. That said, if you are having difficulty getting through your daily life, please contact a licensed health care professional. If you are in danger of harming yourself or others, please contact emergency services immediately.[1]

## Why Now?

Western "civilization" has gone through centuries of persecuting anybody thought to be practicing paranormal activities—to the point of literal witch hunts. For centuries, we have gone through a more rational, scientific age where anything that couldn't be scientifically measured and reproduced was therefore condemned. We are already in a new era where quantum physics is now challenging the mainstream to accept possibilities that were the realm of science fiction just a few decades ago. The rate of change in the world is speeding up, and we are in the middle of changes in human evolution.

We, the authors, are experiencing this change in our own lives. You, the reader, can look back over the years, and we are sure you are noticing how rapidly your realization of your abilities and your capabilities is changing.

Society is changing just as rapidly at a time when the world's richest one percent now has as much wealth as the rest of the world combined. The pace of life has become so fast that many people feel like they are running as quickly as they can in their lives just to keep up. Meanwhile, the media, who thrives on people's fear, is keeping the masses in distress at every level from local to global.

Every major institution is in some form of crisis—government, religion, finance, education, you name it. The old-school approach is no longer working in the way it was intended. It is time for significant changes.

The new era of empaths is part of this change.

## Resources

1. **Emergency Resources**
   Please note that these are mainstream resources and are unlikely to have any understanding of what you mean if you start talking about being an empath.
   http://www.crisistextline.org: Text START to 741-741
   http://www.suicidepreventionlifeline.org: 1-800-273-8255 or Click to Chat from their website.
   Alternatively, dial 911 or your local emergency services.

# CHAPTER 2

# What Is an Empath?

By Trevor

> *Individual human consciousness began with*
> *the illusionary idea of separation.*
> —MOLLY SHEHAN, GREEN HOPE FARM

## Being Empathic Versus Being an Empath

The root of both *empathic* and *empath* comes from the Greek *em* (in) and *pathos* (feeling), but there is a significant difference between the adjective *empathic*, which is widely recognized by the mainstream world, and the noun *empath* which is only now starting to gain recognition.

Being empathic (or empathetic) means a personal identification with the feelings, thoughts, or attitudes of others. Tell me what you are going through, and I can empathize if I have gone through the same or a very similar life experience. The term is usually only used in the context of a conscious awareness between two people who are visually or verbally connected.

Being an empath means having the ability to experience the feelings and emotions of other people as if they were your own. There may be no conscious awareness by you, the empath, of the person whose emotions you are feeling. That person may not even be in the same town, state, or country as you. The emotions may feel like yours. Your mind will try to justify them as yours. You will feel the emotions in your body as if they are yours. But they are NOT yours; they are THEIRS.

If we think those feelings are of our own creation, inevitably we look to fix them. Naturally enough, it is futile to attempt to fix an issue that is not ours to fix.

## Factors Influencing Us as Empaths

There are a number of factors affecting how we pick up energy from other people:

- **Receiving**
  Our sensitivity as receivers will factor into how much energy we pick up.
- **Sending**
  Some people transmit their energy more strongly than others, and the depth of the emotions that they are experiencing will also turn up the volume that they are sending out.
- **Awareness**
  The unaware person may be just as sensitive as the aware person. The latter will understand why they have mood swings; the former will not.
- **Bloodline**
  Blood relatives will affect us regardless of where in the world we are and whether we are thinking about them or not. The link between sender and receiver is often stronger where there is a blood connection. Often, empath children may process the emotions of their parents or siblings long into adulthood.
- **Emotional Connection**
  Friends and acquaintances will impact us primarily based on the strength of the emotional connection we have to them, largely

without regard to physical proximity. The stronger the emotional connection is, the less important the physical proximity is. Having worked from home for many years with teams spread all over the country, I have picked up energy from managers and teammates regardless of location.

- **Physical Proximity**
  Neighbors and strangers will influence us based on physical proximity. This is true for the people living in our neighborhood and the strangers we brush up against in the shopping mall.

## What Being an Empath Is Not!

Let's get this out there now; being an empath has nothing to do with witchcraft, voodoo, 1-800-psychics, mind reading, crazy imagination, cults, or new age religions. It is a perfectly natural state of being. Although only a small percentage of the population have had the conscious experience of being an empath, we believe that most people are capable of it.

Western society has a long history of ridiculing and punishing anyone claiming to have or accused of having abilities that religion could not control or that science could not explain. For sheer self-preservation, these capabilities were driven underground, suppressed, and not discussed. People in the 1900s grew up thinking that anything like this had to be their imagination at best or, worse, a mental illness. Individuals learned to keep it to themselves. The blessed ones were born into families that talked about these things; these abilities tend to follow the bloodline, traditionally (although not exclusively) the female bloodline.

In recent times, talking about being an empath originated in the realm of science fiction. The first use of the word empath was by the sci-fi writer J. T. McIntosh, who published a story called "Empath" in 1956. The TV series *Star Trek* followed, airing the episode "The Empath" in 1968.

Then the world got the Internet.

There are now thousands of people around the world who are starting to find out just how many of us there really are. All it takes is a web search to realize just how widespread this phenomenon is becoming. We can meet each other. We can talk about our experiences. We are not alone.

## Three Stages of Empaths

It is useful to consider three different phases that many empaths experience:

- **The Confused Empath**

  The confused empath spends much of their life overwhelmed. This is primarily caused by either not understanding that they are processing so much from other people or if they do understand, not knowing what to do about it. We wrote this book for you to be able to comprehend who you are, what is happening to you, and especially what to do about it, so you can become a stable empath.

- **The Stable Empath**

  The stable empath understands their tendency to process energy from other people and quickly recognizes when they start taking on that energy. They are in the process of mastering their tools and techniques, and they know that that it takes practice to become a thriving empath. If you are already a stable empath, this book will give you additional processes to help you on your way.

- **The Thriving Empath**

  The thriving empath instinctively recognizes when they are running someone else's energy. They can quickly apply tools and techniques to protect themselves and to help the other person. They are transitioning from becoming a passive, receptive empath to becoming an active healer. The more the thriving empaths help others, the more the empaths will help themselves.

## Scientific Explanations

Some people have incorrectly started associating *mirror neurons* with being an empath. These neurons fire in the brain regardless of whether the subject is performing a particular action or watching someone else perform that same behavior. The neurons mirror the behavior as if the observer were themselves performing the activity. For people who have synesthesia—the experience of one sense when receiving stimulus through a different sense—this can, for instance, cause them to experience tasting food while watching somebody else eating.

However, it is not correct to associate mirror neurons with being an empath. The process does not involve visual proximity. An empath can sense somebody else's emotions regardless of being in the same room or even on the same continent.

Quantum physics is getting closer to understanding empaths with *quantum entanglement*. National Public Radio's show *Invisibilia* explains this well in layman's terms in the January 2015 episode "Entanglement." They start the program with a section on quantum physics and the science of quantum entanglement. They explain that there is a way to "entangle" two atoms separated by space such that an action applied to one instantaneously changes the other.

They interviewed David Hucul, a graduate student at the University of Maryland, who said the following:

> And so far, scientists have been able to get entanglement to occur at a distance of just over eighty-eight miles. Though theoretically you could fly one atom to the moon, and still, if you affected it in some way, the other atom back on Earth would be affected instantaneously in the same way . . . quantum entanglement, the scientists told us, probably happens all the time in the natural world. Like there could be one particle of you right now entangled with a person that you just passed on the street.

Yes, the idea of being entangled with a person you just passed on the street sounds familiar for every empath! Although, more usually, we process the emotions of people we have a connection to: relatives, friends, work colleagues, etc. It doesn't even have to be a positive relationship. The energy involved in disliking, even hating—especially hating—somebody can create the strong bond that enables the empathic connection. As an empath, if you are struggling with negative feelings toward someone, it is more likely that you are picking up on their energy toward you than your real feelings toward them.

Obviously, there is still a lot scientists have to learn and explain if the rest of us are to understand what is happening on the scientific level.

## Frequently Asked Questions of a Newly Aware Empath

When someone first starts to realize that they might be an empath, two questions tend to come up very quickly.

The first is, "How do I know it's not mine?" Our minds are used to creating logical justifications as to why the emotions we are feeling belong to us. Sometimes just challenging that assumption can be enough to dissolve the attachment. If just asking the question "Is it mine?" doesn't release the attachment, then it may be time to use one of the techniques in the chapter "Intuitive Tools and Aids." In particular, muscle testing and pendulum dowsing can be very practical for getting a yes or no answer. You can then determine which group of people you are picking the energy up from: relatives, friends, coworkers, etc. Finally, you can identify a specific individual.

The second question is usually, "How do I protect myself?" Occasionally, when we can intuitively recognize what the emotion is and who it belongs to, it will immediately melt away of its own accord. More often, we need all sorts of other processes to help us do that work. This book provides those tools and techniques.

These pages will help you understand what it means to be an empath and give you tips on turning this ability from a liability into an asset. There may be some techniques we present here that you don't like or that don't work for you. That's okay. Some may take time for you to feel comfortable practicing. A few will feel very natural and will make an immediate difference in your daily life. Try them out and see what works for you.

## The Male Empath

This section (written by Trevor, of course) is dedicated to the minority of our readers, given that female empaths tend to outnumber their male counterparts by at least four to one. Socialization has greater influence on this fact than any physical differences between the sexes because girls are encouraged to be in touch with their emotions and feelings more than boys. By the time they are adults, most men have learned to hide most of their sensitivity.

Why?

Brené Brown, in her book *Daring Greatly*, talks about the ways women and men experience shame in their lives.[1] Women are expected to excel in every area of their lives—looks, mothering, career, relationships, etc.— well beyond anything that is realistic. This is different for men. Brown says, "Basically, men live under the pressure of one unrelenting message: Do not be perceived as weak."

This quote strikes at the core of the male empath if we paraphrase only slightly to say, "Do not be perceived as sensitive!" The opening line of our introductory chapter asks, "Were you described as an 'over-sensitive' child?" because it is a fundamental characteristic of being an empath. When we were young boys, the people around us started to tag us with either being "weakling or strong," "sissy or man," "sensitive or tough."

I know many of the men reading this were labeled with the first of each pair of adjectives. You are unlikely to be reading a book on empaths if you suppressed your sensitivity early in life. Personally, I realized in my thirties that, as early as three years old, I must have thought that the best way to get love and attention from my mother was to play weak and sickly. I was ill throughout most of my childhood years, although needless to say, this strategy did not work too well in my adult life as I tried to climb the corporate ladder. I had to learn to grow up late in life!

It is a conflict in mainstream society to "be a man" and remain an empath. Society teaches us to "man up" in four areas—the four Bs:

- Ballpark – When we first start playing sports as boys, we learn that it is not acceptable to be weak. Crying is totally unacceptable. The ballpark is where defensive lineman in the NFL, Joe Ehrmann, learned "The three scariest words every man receives in his lifetime: Be a man!"
- Bedroom – Some men learn to prove their manliness through their sexual conquests. This objectifies their partners, as they turn their girlfriends into notches on the bedpost. But hey, "Man up!"
- Bank – And if size doesn't work for you anywhere else, there is always the advantage of a fat bank account. Money may not be able to buy you true love, but it will often give you dominance over a woman who is financially dependent on you, and if you are rich enough, it will get you envy from other men, which certainly means you win the challenge to "be a man."
- Bullets – The caveman instinct is to kill or be killed. Even today, the stereotypical man is competitive, the fixer and the protector. He is responsible for looking after his family and is not allowed to be afraid or to ask for support. He must put on a brave face at all times, even to the people closest to him. If all else fails, there is the second amendment right to bear arms.

So what is the antidote?

Look at the four Bs and recognize where you have accepted society's norms in your own life. Do you derive your self-worth as a man from any of these areas? Do you beat yourself up as being less of a man because you haven't succeeded in one or more of them?

An aside here to the women who are reading this section, how do you support these old stereotypes as expectations for the men in your life? What do you require of them so you can be the woman you think you ought to be? There are many wives and girlfriends who expect their men to conform to these outdated concepts because their own self-identity requires them to be in a relationship with a "real man."

Men, it is time to change the basis for our self-worth!

Joe Ehrmann went on to become a pastor championing a redefinition of what it means to be a man. In a 2014 interview, he was asked for his own version of manhood and replied, "I think it could be only defined by two things. One, it's your capacity to love and to be loved. Masculinity ought to be defined in terms of relationships. Second thing, it ought to be defined by commitment to a cause—that all of us have a responsibility to give back—to make the world more fair, more just, more hospitable for every human being." [2]

As male empaths, we are well along that road. We know what it feels like to truly connect with other people, and because of that, we are regularly developing our capacity to love and be loved.

The second part of Ehrmann's definition, "that all of us have a responsibility to give back," may be more challenging for many, yet we have an advantage. As empaths, we are born healers in ways that few non-empaths are. How we give back may look very different for each of us, and any difficulty is most likely to be in finding our own unique path. Yet I believe that whether we are male or female, to fully thrive as empaths, we have to find our way to contribute. More about this in the final chapter, "Thriving as Healers in a Changing World."

## It Is an Asset, Not a Liability

Remember, the greater the emotional sensitivity, the greater the challenge of trying to operate in mainstream society.

So many empaths have felt cursed by this ability. You can liken it to a car: A car can be used to visit friends, or it can cause accidents by speeding or texting while driving. The answer is not to give up using a car, but rather to know how to use it properly.

When we don't know how to use our abilities, we are out of control. Once we understand them, they become useful tools that have the potential to be used to help the people around us and ourselves.

## Empaths in Organizations

The best consultants will tell you that as they moved from one company to another, they became skilled in quickly identifying the corporate culture of their clients. Each company has a unique personality that reflects the people in it, especially its leaders.

In my early days of learning about my abilities as an empath, I found out about corporate cultures firsthand. At the time, I was living in a nice house with my wife and two young children; we were a happy family with everything going for us. I got up one particular morning, had breakfast, kissed them all goodbye, and drove my luxury car to my six-figure job. As I parked in the garage next to the office, I had every reason to feel successful and upbeat. Yet as I walked from the parking lot through the main doors into the office building, I noticed that I began to feel like a failure—an emotion I felt all too often at my workplace.

"What is wrong with me?" I asked myself.

At that moment, I realized the corporate culture of the organization I was working for. It was one of "We'll get the best work out of you if we keep you off balance and feeling insecure." It was a false philosophy, of course, but one that was rampant, and encouraged, among the executive management. I had bought into the lie, but once I had seen behind the proverbial curtain, I would never buy into it again. It put me on a mission to talk to my friends who were having the same difficulties in the office and say, "Of course you feel like a failure at work. Of course you feel insecure. It has nothing to do with you. It's the corporate culture based on wanting you to feel like that."

Many of you reading this may be realizing for the first time that you have been buying into a scenario like this in your life. It may not be at the office; it may be at church or school or any organization with which you associate. Anywhere there is a social identity, there will be an emotional culture that may overwhelm you. It won't be in the mission statement or on the marketing pamphlet, but you will hear it and feel it loud and clear. Once you identify the pattern, it will lose its power over you; then use the Light Projector exercise in the chapter "Shielding" to keep yourself insulated.

## Empaths and Religion

People have asked about whether there is a conflict between being an empath and religion. Of course, if you indiscriminately follow any particular religious leader, even your local minister, you are giving away your personal power to them. If that person holds an unfavorable view of empaths, then indeed there is a conflict regardless of what we say here.

However, if you want to make up your own mind about this question, the following guidance regarding society's evolution from control to partnerships may help.

People have created controlling communities since Sumerian civilization in 4,000 BC or earlier. Over thousands of years, human interaction based on controlling others has developed unsustainable greed to a point where the planet itself may not be viable for many more generations. What was replaced can still be seen today in what is left of the planet's indigenous people who live in partnership societies. The idea of a small percentage of the population controlling a vast portion of society's wealth is insanity to native tribes. What we are seeing around us today are the early signs of controlling societies crumbling. Institutions are set up to monitor the people within their sphere of influence. As the planet evolves, people are increasingly intolerant of being controlled. All of the civil unrest around the world is reflecting a global trend toward resisting control.

At the level of our personal relationships, how do we interact with others around us? Is it on a basis of who can control who, with a winner-takes-all outcome? Or is it by mutual empowerment, where the only acceptable outcome is a win-win for all involved parties?

The temptation to give our power away is deeply embedded in our societies; from our parents and our schoolteachers to our religious leaders, spiritual counselors, doctors, and financial advisors, most of us were taught from an early age to yield to authority. Specifically from a religious viewpoint, ask yourself, "Does religion try to control me or empower me?" To be more precise, "Do the practitioners try to control me or empower me? Do they pretend to empower me by teaching me how to conform while speaking of freedom? What feelings do they engender in me?" Regardless of their words, if they speak of love but there is a tightness in your gut, ask yourself if they are instilling fear.

On the level of society, we are approaching full circle by coming back to partnership, from control. On the level of the individual, the rising awareness in empaths can be seen as a development from separation to oneness. Concurrent with that, the individual level is learning to trust what we are experiencing in our own bodies rather than what other people tell us we cannot or should not be experiencing.

The Native Americans have a story of having a wolf on each shoulder, a bad wolf on one, a good wolf on the other. The bad wolf represents fear, hate, and greed. The good wolf represents love, compassion, and hope. Which is going to win? The one you are choosing to feed!

## Terminology

As society changes, so does its language. The world is waking up to emotional intelligence (EQ) as consciousness rises in the world, but the vocabulary associated with being an empath is often confused. For someone who is developing their abilities, it is useful to distinguish between the following terms:

- Empath – Someone who has the ability to experience the feelings and emotions of other people. Occasionally, this may include experiencing another's physical symptoms as well. This ability may exist regardless of the physical proximity, the range of the five physical senses, or any intellectual knowledge of the activities of the other person.
- Highly Sensitive Person (HSP) – Empaths may be considered a group within HSPs. Being highly sensitive may or may not include empathic abilities, as an HSP may only have extreme sensitivity to some or all of the recognized five senses. HSPs may also be able to read other people with whom they have physical contact, to a degree far beyond that of the average person. An empath may be influenced by other people regardless of any physical connection.
- Intuitive – Someone who is intuitive can have an instinctive sense of what is appropriate for themselves or someone else. Sometimes this referred to as being sensitive. This awareness does not necessarily include an empathic connection of feeling another person's emotions. A medical intuitive is someone who can provide a medical diagnosis for another person, either in their presence or remotely.
- Medium – A medium is someone who serves as a middle person, usually between living people and deceased souls, but this may also extend to other dimensional beings. Communication with disembodied beings is in no way associated with being an empath.
- Channeling – This is the process a medium uses to connect with other dimensional beings while in a trance state. Again, this is not part of being an empath.
- Clair Senses – There are distinct terms for the ways in which different people experience their psychic abilities. *Clair sense* is a

term covering all of the inner senses. The most common are the following:

- Clairvoyance – clear or inner seeing; receiving information in the form of pictures or symbols.
- Clairaudience – clear or inner hearing; listening to a voice or voices.
- Clairsentience – clear or inner feeling; getting sensations in the body.
- Claircognizance – clear or inner knowing; receiving information in a way that is beyond any describable inner sense. People experiencing information in this way often say, "Don't ask me how I know. I just know."

Empaths operate primarily with claircognizance and clairsentience (also referred to as clairempathy). Because these abilities are so far removed from mainstream understanding, there is still much confusion over these terms. These four clairs are the most common, although any of the basic five senses can be used in a psychic context.

- Psychic – Possibly the most misused term of all of the above and is best understood as being the use of any extrasensory perception (ESP). In other words, anybody with unexplained mental talents can be considered to be psychic, although this term is often misused to be synonymous with the term *medium*. Strictly speaking, all mediums are psychic, but not all psychics are mediums.

## Other Abilities You May Have

It is common for empaths to have additional extrasensory abilities as well as being able to connect to other people's emotions. While mediumship and channeling are not part of being an empath, these are skills that may appear alongside your empathic abilities.

The following are some of the many other talents you may start to discover for yourself:

- Seeing auras – The ability to see energy in and around another person.
- Precognition – Knowing about events that will happen in the future.
- Remote seeing – The ability to know what is currently happening in a distant place.
- Psychometry – Being able to tell the history of an object or its owner by holding it.
- Animal communication – The ability to speak to and hear pets and other animals.
- Plant communication – Picking up information from plants, often in the form of understanding how they can be used for medicinal purposes.
- Elemental empaths – People who can feel the forces and physical processes that affect the earth.

As you become more accepting of your abilities as an empath, these other talents may become stronger. Of course, there are plenty of non-empaths who have these experiences, just as there are many empaths who do not have these other skills. The purpose of this book is not to discuss any of these other abilities in detail. However, if you are experiencing any of these traits, you are still a perfectly normal empath. The exercises described here will help you balance all your gifts along with your empathic abilities.

## Resources

1. *Daring Greatly: How the Courage to Be Vulnerable Transforms the Way We Live, Love, Parent, and Lead* by Brené Brown
2. "The 3 Scariest Words a Boy Can Hear" on National Public Radio's *All Things Considered*, July 14, 2014

# CHAPTER 3

# Our Stories

## We Are All Connected

By Trevor

In a world of Internet connectivity and the global village, the fact that we are all connected is almost a cliché. But I am going to give you a different spin on that phrase sharing my own experiences.

Let me start with a recent incident. For four days in a row, I had been feeling unpleasant emotions that I identified as belonging to a friend from my corporate work, even though she lives at the other end of the country. The intensity and the recurrence were such that I knew it was something serious. I had had no communication with her for a couple of weeks, before I spoke to her on the fourth day. As soon as she picked up the phone, I said "Okay, you are having a horrible week, and in fact, I am surprised that you are even working." Even though she knew much of my story that I am about to share here, her confirming response was an almost sheepish "How did you know?" before filling me in on all of the details of what had been happening in her world.

This was not an isolated experience. In fact, these experiences now occur almost daily.

I am an empath.

I am able to experience other people's emotions in my own body, so I really know when someone is having a horrible week.

I first remember hearing the word empath in the late 1980s in the context of watching Deanna Troi, the star ship's counselor on *Star Trek: The Next Generation*. It was to be another twenty-five years before I would consider using the term to describe myself.

In the early 1990s, I was working at my desk around mid-morning. I felt hungry and thought, "My stomach thinks it's lunch time, but it's only ten o'clock." At that moment, the woman sitting opposite me looked up and said, "I'm starving. I missed breakfast this morning." It was at that moment that I knew something interesting was happening to me.

During the following years, I became increasingly aware that the people around me were influencing my emotions, especially work colleagues, even though I was working from home. I still didn't think of myself as an empath, but I wrote myself a reminder that I put near my desk that read "It's not your stuff. Be aware."

This brings us to the summer of 2012. July was an emotionally difficult month for me, full of self-doubt and confusion. I got to the end of the month and realized that the emotions I was struggling with were not my own. In that moment, I realized who the emotions really belonged to and what those emotions were, and with that, they melted away. It was an incredible release. Most of August, however, followed a similar pattern until I again recognized the emotions I was processing and to whom they belonged. Well, I must be a slow learner. I repeated the same pattern a third time through most of September, and at that point, I remembered about Deanna Troi and realized, "I am an empath."

I have known empaths who considered their ability a curse. At this stage in 2012, I knew it was a gift, an untrained gift but nevertheless a gift. I went looking for training.

That December, one of my alternative health care providers practiced a new form of energy healing on me. The next day I phoned a friend of mine in Dallas and told her about this new mode of healing. I offered to practice it on her over the phone. To my surprise, she got it immediately and could feel the impact; I was off! This was my transition from being a receptive empath to being able to use my abilities for remote energy healing.

For the next few weeks, I worked with two people a day, mostly friends and relatives, but I wanted volume. I knew that the way of becoming an expert was to work on as many people as possible. After a few months, I started working with complete strangers over the Internet, usually knowing nothing about them other than a name.

There is a subtle difference between being empathic and being an empath. Being empathic means a personal identification with the feelings, thoughts, or attitudes of others. Tell me about what you are going through, and I can empathize. Being an empath, especially in terms of being an unskilled empath, means taking on the feelings, thoughts, or attitudes of others as if they were one's own—even before there is any conscious awareness of what is happening. Empaths experience feelings in the body; it is our minds that create a justification for why we feel a particular way.

I first noticed how insidious the mind can be, for myself, on the occasion of one of the early times I sat down to work remotely on someone I didn't know. I had already created a procedure that I still follow each time I work with someone new. As I sat down to work on this person, let's call him Jim, I began to feel angry. Immediately, I started thinking about the cable company that was giving me terrible customer service. I was angry at this organization to the point that I thought, "Okay, Jim's going to have to wait. Enough. I need to write them another letter." I stopped myself and realized that the anger I felt at that moment had nothing to do with me nor the cable company, but everything to do with the energy I was picking up from Jim. I was feeling his anger, and my brain wanted to find a rational reason for why I was feeling angry.

At this stage, the information I was tuning into was becoming more and more personal. It surprised me the first time I told a woman what had happened to her and how old she was when it happened. She was a complete stranger to me, I only knew her first and last name, and we were corresponding through email. I had written that she had been sixteen at the time of the incident. Her email reply corrected me slightly and said it was actually just before her sixteenth birthday, but she confirmed that indeed, it wasn't rape, but the only reason that was true was that she didn't know she was supposed to say no to her stepfather.

That was a shock to me. It is a responsibility to be given that much insight into somebody's private life, although I honestly believe I am only given appropriate information for the other person. It serves as proof to a new client that I know what I am doing as an energy healer. Often when these type of exchanges happen, I give them part of the story, and they then tell me the rest. The whole purpose is one of healing, but it still feels odd to receive intuitive insights into somebody's deeply intimate life details.

My abilities as an empath are continuing to grow daily. Although, just in case you are concerned about meeting me or other empaths, this still isn't anything I can do at will. I have no control over when this happens and for whom. I can't decide to find out all the juicy details about whom I choose when I choose. Bottom line, your privacy is still safe however much you are a close friend or complete stranger to me. This is almost certainly true about all the empaths in your life. They may not know the details about why you are feeling emotional; they will likely know *when* and *what* you are feeling emotionally.

My experience is that human connectivity is not limited by physical distance, by town, by state, by continent. The more I share my experiences, the more I realize how many people around the world are experiencing this state of being for themselves. I know this is a new idea for many of you who are not empaths. I simply ask you to entertain the possibility that, in whole new ways you may never have thought possible, *we are all connected.*

## Am I an Empath? . . . What Is an Empath?
By Abbigayle

I didn't hear the term empath until I was twenty-nine years old. Of course, I knew what it meant to be empathetic or to show empathy for someone. I often found myself wondering why more people weren't simply better at connecting with others. However, the idea that there was an entire community who could process other people's physical and emotional energy was an entirely foreign concept to me. I had plenty of evidence that this was exactly what I was doing, though at the time I had nothing to compare it to in my private corner of Nowhere, Georgia.

When I was six years old, my mother became pregnant with my little sister. At the time, I was living almost sixty miles away at my grandparent's home, and I caught what my German grandmother deemed *der morgan grippe* (morning flu). I would wake in the mornings with horrible nausea and developed an acute sensitivity to smells for nearly two months. Then, just as suddenly as it came, it was gone. In hindsight, I was struck by this "morgan grippe" every time someone close to me was with child. Morning sickness was but one of the many "joys of motherhood" I vicariously experienced.

I was always keenly aware of the fact that my life seemed to be a constant game of emotional "monkey see monkey do." I had no idea why it happened; I only knew that if someone else felt a certain way, then, like it or not, I was sure to follow. A perfect example of this was when I was in second grade; my most aggressive bully announced to the class that she and her family were moving to Kentucky. Internally, I was thrilled! Never again would she be there to lead the other girls in a chorus of "Scabby Abbey!" Maybe with her gone, the other girls would just get bored and leave me alone. My relief was short lived though, because she was a very popular girl, and most of the class, in contrast to me, was pretty devastated by her departure. By the end of the day, a dark cloud had settled in my heart. Why did I feel so sad? By the time I was off the school bus, my body was in the throes of a full-blown panic attack. My grandmother called these emotional overloads "hysterics" and berated me for "having feelings for someone such as that." I had no way of explaining then what my imaginary friends explained as best they could: that I wasn't having these feelings FOR her. I was having them WITH her.

I was a smart kid and quickly learned that if I got too close to people, inevitably they were going to make me feel "yucky" or "gross." (I still haven't outgrown using either term when describing the way I sense heavy or negative energy.) So, instead of subjecting myself to that ickiness, I emotionally stayed as far away from people as I could, retreating instead to the safety of the solitude of my mind.

Twenty years later, I was working on a group project for college and gave my partner a quick call. It lasted less than ten minutes, but it changed the course of my life forever.

"I just wanted to let you know that I'll be turning the project in tomorrow. Even though you haven't said it, I know you weren't happy with the last slide changes, so I went ahead and switched it back. Don't worry, I don't think the team even looked at it, so they won't care." I was stunned by the awkward silence I heard on the other line. Then he just started laughing. "I didn't even mention the slide. How did you know? That's the third time you've known what I was thinking before I even had a chance to bring it up. Plus, you call me every single time I'm thinking about the project. You know, I think you might be an empath. You should Google it because you're not the only one, and they might be able to teach you how to live with it."

Within forty-eight hours I had joined an online empath community chat room and posed the question that had been burning in my brain my whole life: "Am I crazy or am I an empath? And by the way, WTF is an empath?" Over the next few weeks, I devoured any information I could find. From crystals and indigo children (something else I had never heard of but quickly learned that I certainly fit the bill) to guardian angels and spirit guides. All of this was like quenching my thirst at an oasis in the desert and wondering all these years, "What am I? Why am I so different? Why can't I just get a grip? Why can't I ever just feel NORMAL . . . ?" Eventually, I reached out to a mentorship group on the Empath Community looking for a teacher and received a vague-sounding reply from a man named Trevor Lewis. He offered to do something he called emotion clearing. I read his introduction to the process and thought to myself, "This is WAY too easy; there must be a catch." But I was completely open to the idea of it, even if I was doubtful that it would work. Nevertheless, though, if this dude claimed he could get the nightmares and monsters out of my head then, "Yes! Yes! A thousand times yes!"

# CHAPTER 4

# Visualization and The Power of Intent

By Trevor

*An object imbued with intent—it has power,*
*it's treasure, we're drawn to it.*
—John Charles Hockenberry

## Visualization Works

Most top athletes in every sport use visualization techniques. They're an important part of sports training. Mental coaches would say they're the key to peak performance in almost every discipline in life. If these techniques works for top performers, it only makes sense to apply them to ourselves in our everyday lives.

We discussed mirror neurons in the section on "Scientific Explanations" in the chapter "What Is an Empath?" The neural pathways in our mind do not recognize the difference between seeing someone else performing a task and performing that task ourselves. Similarly, when we go through the process of visualization, our mind cannot distinguish between seeing ourselves perform the action in our mind and actively performing the task with our physical body.

What is true physically is also true mentally, emotionally, and spiritually. Visualization processes and imagination techniques can work at all levels of our being to help us perform better in all parts of our life.

This book is full of visualization techniques to help you become a thriving empath.

## People Learn Differently

People process information in different ways. Some people take in information visually through their eyes, others auditorily through their ears, and the third group kinesthetically through their bodies. For a classroom full of students to learn a topic in an all-encompassing manner, the teacher has to include seeing, hearing, and doing. By doing, a student will get it in his or her body and feel what it is like to learn. The top advertising agencies use this to their full advantage by targeting all three channels in their marketing efforts.

Most people have a dominant channel, and their choice of vocabulary usually reflects this. Compare the phrases "I see what you mean," "I hear what you're saying," and "I feel touched by what you're saying." Same meaning, but the different phraseology emphasizes the different sensory channel used for processing the information. In addition, the visual person tends to talk faster, have a slimmer body type, and if they make hand gestures as they speak, it will tend to be at and above shoulder level. The kinesthetic person tends to talk slower, have a heavier body type, and make hand gestures at waist level and below. The auditory person is somewhere in the middle. Of course, these are all generalizations meant as guidelines only.

What is your dominant channel?

You probably already know. If not, think about your own learning mode. For instance, when you need directions from somebody (or some app) do you need to look at the map or listen to instructions? Maybe, if you are kinesthetic, you prefer to go to the destination once and then you have the route in your body.

It is useful to recognize your preferred learning channel. Visual people take in information very quickly; after all, a picture is worth a thousand words. Visual people may think that they cannot do guided meditations because when the facilitator starts talking, they will get a visual immediately. By the time the facilitator continues to speak for several minutes, visual learners can become so bored or confused that they are convinced that that they are doing something wrong or that guided meditations don't work. The kinesthetic learner takes more time to integrate new information and, in turn, can have longer retention.

Naturally, the exercises entitled "visualizations" are going to emphasize the visual channel. If you are auditory or kinesthetic, consider if you need to adapt the processes so that you hear more or feel more. The more important techniques, especially The Light Projector exercise, have already been tailored to make this easier for everybody.

## Releasing Concentration

With all of these mental exercises, it's not about HOLDING a thought, it's about FOCUSING a thought. One analogy is to treat the mind like an active child when you want them to sit still. You are going to tell them to stay where they are, but sooner or later they will get distracted and start wandering off. You bring them back, they sit still for a while, and then the process starts all over again. When your mental attention wanders off from the subject of focus, gently bring it back. Keep repeating the process. Just bring your attention back to your subject. Do not worry about having thoughts; they are natural. Do not try. Let it be . . . easy!

You'll see this theme repeated as a reminder in some of the exercises below. It's that important.

## The Power of Intent

The most important part of any of the exercises shared here is the intent that they are going to work. Some people teach some of the details of the exercises in a polar opposite way to the way we present them here. They still work just as well. Intention is at least 80 percent of the reason most techniques work. The details of the processes are only 20 percent of their effectiveness.

## An Exercise—Your Inner Garden

Let's start with an easy visualization process to get you warmed up.

Your Inner Garden is a place you can imagine for yourself, to go and recuperate from any stresses of the day. You can also use it to create anything you want to create in your life. For you, it may be a beach or a meadow. Your Inner Garden is yours to design as you wish with trees, flowers, swings, benches, ponds, and lakes. As you spend more time in it, you can change for the better anytime you wish. If you create your desires in your Inner Garden, then, like all visualizations, your subconscious doesn't recognize the difference between imagined and real and will work toward manifesting in the real world whatever it is you wish for. For this reason, many people keep money trees in their Inner Garden, where money does grow on trees and can be plucked like fruit.

If you are more auditory or kinesthetic, what sounds can you hear in this space? How does your Inner Garden make you feel? Maybe even ask yourself what you can taste and smell there.

Sit comfortably. Close your eyes. Take a few deep breaths, and spend a few minutes with your own Inner Garden. You may want to write down a few notes afterward about what you created.

Have fun and know that there are no wrong answers for this exercise!

# CHAPTER 5

# Shielding

By Abbigayle

*Your spirit is the true shield.*
—MORIHEI UESHIBA

Shielding ourselves against unwanted energy or emotions from others is a vital part of taking care of ourselves as empaths. Being around other people is THE biggest challenge for most empaths, and learning to shield effectively can be life changing.

In a world where we are constantly connected to others around us, within our physical space or through Internet, television, smartphones, etc., we are energetically tethered to one another in ways undocumented in history. This ability to connect 24/7 with the snap of a finger is a double-edged sword. Yes, it gives us the ability to connect with other empaths and lightworkers from all over the world in ways that would never happen without the technology of today. But the downside is that we are now making ourselves available to an infinite barrage of emotional energy, often with little warning. You can become swept up in a whirlpool of feelings simply by logging into social media. It becomes even more necessary in a modern society of constant connection to develop healthy shielding practices, not just for face-to-face interaction with someone, but for keeping boundaries within cyber energy as well. There are as many techniques as there are empaths, but the following are among the most common:

- A lot of people find it useful in the beginning to envision themselves wrapped in an invisible bubble of energy or being behind a wall where unwanted emotions or energy cannot pass. This can be especially useful when you know you are particularly susceptible— for instance, with certain people, at a family event, or even in a crowded grocery store.

- Others find it more helpful to envision themselves safe within a bottle (think of it like a genie's bottle; once inside it opens up to a big, safe space). Within this bottle, you are fully aware of the present moment and can process nothing but your own energy. Picture a white light coming in through the bottle, erasing any unwanted or negative residue within your system.

- Some people prefer the practice of visualizing a wall or mirror that the unwanted stuff can bounce off of "like BBs off a Buick." This is the empath version of the childhood saying, "I'm rubber, you're glue; whatever you say bounces off me and sticks to you." When we have other people's stuff projected toward us, our initial response is to soak it up like a sponge. Instead, visualize it as bouncing off, redirecting the energy back to its source. We will discuss another way of doing this when we cover releasing.

At times, it can also be useful to be able to control how much you are or aren't picking up. Perhaps you want to be able to connect with someone, but you don't want it rushing through your system as if it's your own. Then the volume controls are imperative. Picture a box with three knobs; one is labeled My Self-talk, another My Higher Self, and the third Other People. Picture each knob having notches from 10 percent to 100 percent. You can adjust the "volume" or the feedback that you receive simply by adjusting the knob. If you notice that someone is overwhelming you with their emotions but you don't want to "cut them off," you can take a moment to turn your reception of their flow down some and adjust your own volume accordingly. If you want to spend time with your higher self, you can turn your self-talk volume down significantly, but remember to turn it back up again when you finish. Your self-talk is there to keep you safe in the world. When that voice sounds negative, ask it how it is trying to protect you, rather than shutting it off.

Up until now, we have been taking a defensive approach to sensitivity; most shielding is about keeping the bad stuff out. Trevor has developed a more proactive approach to this particular subject. The Light Projector exercise is less about what's coming in and more about what you are putting out.

## Gridding

Gridding is a way of providing a shield against unwanted energies entering your home or workplace. You can create grids using the following process:

1. For each grid, you will need four metal objects. Pennies are wonderfully convenient and hold an energetic charge well.

2. Determine where you are going to place your grids; we recommend a minimum of four nested levels. If you are gridding a home, start outside with the boundaries of the land in a rectangular pattern with four right-angled corners. The next grid will be immediately around the outside of the building. The third will be at the room level for each room you want to grid. Pick the ones where you spend the most time: your bedroom, your office, etc. The fourth level will be around your personal space in that room: your bed, your desk, and so on. You can add grids for each room you want to protect. You can even add grids around your doorways and windows.

3. Set your intention for the coins (four coins for each grid) by holding them in your hand and declaring, "I charge you all with working

together to energetically guard and protect this space from all dark or dense energy for the highest good of all concerned." You can amend and extend the wording as you feel appropriate. How would you give instructions to a human team of spiritually-minded security guards if you were hiring them to protect your home? You can specify your family member's names. You can add explicit time frames, for example, every day of every week, twenty-four hours a day. Add whatever feels right for you.

4. Starting with the outermost grid, the one around the outside of the property, place one coin in each corner of the rectangle. Secure each coin so as to be undisturbed over time. Repeat for each grid moving inward.

## The Light Projector Exercise

By Trevor

The following exercise is THE number one core practice that I share with other empaths.

One of the themes that I discovered as I have worked with hundreds of different people is that we suffer as empaths when we are only in receptor mode. We thrive as empaths when we step into healer mode. This exercise doesn't resonate for everybody, but it seems to work for the vast majority, and for some, it has been life changing. Before using this technique, some empaths were unable to go even to the supermarket or a restaurant because they were so sensitive to other people's energy. By using this exercise, they have been able to go back out in public again. For others, it's just a way of staying "clean" when interacting with other people. Personally, I use it every day. I hope you use it and enjoy it.

The analogy I use is of two barrels of water. If a barrel of dirty water feeds through a pipe into a barrel of clean water, the clean water starts to look as dirty as the water in the dirty barrel. If the water flows in the other direction, the dirty water gets cleaner, and the clean water is still clean. By refilling from the Divine wellspring, the clean barrel is refreshed.

Most shielding exercises we use as empaths turn off the flow of water, and we know what eventually happens to stagnant water when it sits for too long! When we operate as healers, we keep the flow of water moving from the clean barrel to the dirty barrel.

When we operate only in receptor mode, we are picking up other people's "dirty water." Not only that, but also our first instinct is to think that if we feel bad, it must be something about us. Our minds look to justify why any emotion we are feeling must be our own and then work out how to fix it. It's  the result of growing up in a mechanistic world that teaches us we are all separate. As empaths, we know how untrue this is. We are all connected, and that is true regardless of distance. For me, learning that I was processing other people's emotions was, in itself, the first huge step forward. Then, as I cleared myself of my own emotional baggage, I was better able to recognize when I was processing other people's emotions. In fact, once I realized that emotions were often not my own, I was able to ask whose emotions were passing through me and what those emotions were. Once I can identify whose emotions I am processing, and especially once I can identify what emotions they are, those emotions usually drop away, and I go back to feeling myself again. Even though I know this works, there are still times when I don't remember to ask the question, is this mine? It is easy to fall into the trap of immediately assuming it is our own.

So how do we move from being passive receptors to being active healers? A friend was dreading going to a funeral because, as an empath, she knew all of the emotions she was going to pick up. I "downloaded" the following exercise by way of an answer to her. She said it worked like a charm! I now recommend doing this to avoid taking on other people's energy and as protection from being drained by being around others.

**Practicing the Light Projector Exercise**

1.  Start off by grounding. Imagine roots coming out from under your feet and going deep down into the center of the earth.
2.  You are a Light Projector, a conduit of Divine Energy.

    The process is to channel Divine Light, Divine Energy, and send it out to the people in your environment. This point is important: If you send your energy out, it will be exhausting for you. It will drain you and weaken you even more, causing you to let in even more of their energy when your defenses are down. You are only a ***conduit*** for Universal Light.

    I have presented this exercise in three different forms below for people who are primarily visual, auditory, or kinesthetic (feeling). Use whatever style or combination works best for you.

    a.  **Visual**

        Visualize the energy in the form of light coming in through the top of your head, down your spine, all the way to your feet, filling your whole body, and then out from your heart to them. The flow of Divine Energy through you and out to your environment will help to push their energy away from you. Also, just as a water pipe cannot channel water without getting wet, you will be energized by the flow of Divine Energy through you. It may help to visualize the energy coming into your head as white light, and send it out of your heart as a prism of rainbow-colored light.

b. **Auditory**

Bring the energy through the top of your head as an *ee* sound (internally within yourself or externally by actually making a sound). Send it down your spine all the way to your feet, filling your whole body, and then send it out from your heart as an *oo* to them. Inhale on the *ee*, and exhale on the *oo*.

c. **Kinesthetic (feeling)**

Feel the waves of energy coming in through the top of your head as a vibration of love. Think of the warm and fuzzy feeling of playing with puppies or kittens. Send it down your spine all the way to your feet, filling your whole body, and then send it out from your heart.

3. You want to keep that flow going into your environment 24/7. Keep that up consciously for a short while; then just have the intention of keeping the flow going. Tell your subconscious that this is what you want to be doing 24/7, and then let go. Check in occasionally, when you remember, so as to keep the process going. Keeping the flow of Divine Energy down through you and out to the people around you is the best form of shielding.

4. Do not concentrate. The mind will get distracted. All you need to do is gently bring your attention back to the exercise. When the subject of a photo moves out of focus, all you do is refocus the lens of the camera. When the object of your mental attention moves out of focus, refocus the mind. Just bring your attention back to your subject. Do not worry about having thoughts. Do not try. Let it be . . . easy!

5. You can use it for a single person who may be annoying you. You can use it for a room full of people (such as a work meeting) or a whole building. Especially with a crowd, it is much better to use this exercise before you leave home and before you are entering their space. Once you walk into the building and you start to take

on their energy, the momentum of the flow is already moving from them to you. This exercise will help, but it is harder to reverse the direction of the flow of energy. It is far better to create the flow through you to them from the outset.

**Experiences with the Light Projector Exercise**

Here is a quote from an empath friend on her initial use of this exercise:

*Yesterday I imagined being a light projector every time I left my house, and it immediately made me calm. I even went to the store yesterday alone without my husband and kids, who I usually use as a buffer between other people and me. This morning I imagined being a projector before getting out of bed, and I've been in a good mood since. It seems to calm me whenever I'm about to go bananas.*

Some of my thriving empath friends have been doing their own version of this exercise for some time. For example, one responded as follows

*This is something I came to realize myself a little while ago. Each day, I ask to be used as a conduit of Divine Light and Love to this world. I ask that Divine Love be infused within my spirit and body, that it flow out to everyone I meet on that day and out to everyone they meet so that the Light will flow outward and elevate this world into the higher frequencies. I can feel it flow down through the top of my head, across my shoulders, and down into my legs, exiting through my feet and connecting to the earth. I find that if I am in continuous "send" mode that negative energy has no chance to come into my life. If I do have someone of a negative charge come into my day, they will have little to no effect on me. It feels like the positive aura around me just flows over them and has a calming effect on them.*

For myself, as an intuitive healer and coach, being an empath is extremely useful. It is an ability that I want to keep and control and, indeed, even amplify. What I started to realize, though, was that I didn't have an off switch. I particularly realized this when I woke up one morning processing some emotion that didn't feel like mine. I asked whether it was mine, and got a no. I asked whether it belonged to a member of my family; again no. I got a yes when I asked if it belonged to a client, and I proceeded to test whose emotion it was and what the emotion was. I then cleared the person and emailed her that I had just cleared her for "confusion" and quickly got a reply back: "*Thank goodness. I was processing that all night.*" What I have now done is set an intention for office hours and emergencies only. In other words, I turn on my empathic listening only when I am doing healing work, unless someone is having an emergency, in which case, I am willing to be interrupted

This exercise is the first step toward moving from being an unconscious empath to a conscious one. In the final chapter, "From Empaths to Healers in a Changing World," we will go into more details on becoming a healer. First, however, let's talk more about ways to look after ourselves as empaths.

# CHAPTER 6

# Grounding

By Abbigayle

> *To ground is to pour your energies back into the earth*
> *and feel the warm calm of nature in exchange.*
> —UNKNOWN

## What is Grounding?

Grounding simply means connecting your energy to the earth. We have chosen to take on human bodies, and when we disconnect from our bodies, we are disconnecting our energy from the earth. To be in balance, we need to be connected upward to the Divine and downward to the earth so that life-energy can flow through us. This way we stay centered and healthy.

It is our intention that you pick and choose from the exercises we have included here. You will feel that some are more effective than others. Which ones should you use for starters? Go back to trusting your intuition! Some will seem more useful on some days, under some circumstances, while others will work better on different occasions.

Just remember, grounding is a critical skill for empaths. Whenever you feel off center, these exercises are a great place to start the recentering process.

## 5-4-3-2-1

This exercise is ideal as an emergency drill. Use it when you are off-center and need to reconnect quickly with who you are. Consciously connect with each of your senses. Count off each of the following:

- 5 things you can see
- 4 things you can feel
- 3 things you can hear
- 2 things you can smell
- 1 thing you love about yourself

The purpose is to get you back in your body and reconnected with yourself in the present moment. In the process, as you put more attention on yourself in the here and now, you will de-emphasize regrets about the past, fears about the future, and any emotional flack that you are picking up from the people around you.

## Rooting

In Tai Chi, the concept of *rooting* literally means being connected to the ground. In many forms of martial arts, being grounded energetically and being grounded physically are one and the same. So, groundedness of mind reflects in groundedness of body.

Begin by standing with your feet together. Take several long, deep breaths, and then move your right foot so your feet are shoulder length apart. Imagine you are growing roots from your legs, through the soles of your feet, deep down into the center of the earth. The roots are flexible, so you can lift your feet without disconnecting. Now return to your first stance with feet together. Take several long breaths and move your left foot so your feet are again shoulder length apart. Feel the roots stabilizing your body, holding you firmly to the ground. Once you can transition smoothly from each position, practice moving around some while maintaining the deep-rooted connection you have with the ground. Practice at home first so you are able to do it while you carry on a conversation. It may feel a little weird at first to do this while you are in any form of moving vehicle, but that will pass with practice! It's your imagination; make it work for you, and keep practicing.

## Back to Nature

> Nature is fuel for the soul. Often when we feel depleted
> we reach for a cup of coffee, but research suggests a
> better way to get energized is to connect with nature
> —Richard Ryan, professor of psychology
> at the University of Rochester.

There is a natural order in nature that can be lost in the chaos of mainstream living. To reconnect with nature, take a walk in the woods and maybe even hug a tree while you're there. Or, if that's a little too extreme, just sit against a tree and enjoy its company for a while. Getting out into nature is one of the easiest and simplest ways to ground oneself. It just makes you feel alive again to step into a cool breeze or a warm ray of sunshine. Sunshine provides a natural source of energy, rich in nutrients that all play a significant role in mental health and brain function. Spending time outside also increases our oxygen levels, which has many additional benefits, not the least of which is a reduction in anxiety and healthier blood pressure. Any time outside helps, especially gardening or doing things that immerse your hands in nature.

Taking your shoes off and connecting with the energy of the earth for even just five minutes can equally bring you back to center. If you are unable to do this for some reason, rooting is the next best thing. By just envisioning your roots running deep within the earth and drawing from its energetic source, you can ground yourself to approach a situation more clearly.

When you are outside, pay particular attention to the things that bring you the most joy, and try to incorporate these into your living space as much as possible. For example, if you have a special affection for the mountains, then perhaps take a few pictures from your favorite view and have one of them turned into a canvas painting for your office. If you love gardening, perhaps some silk flowers on your coffee table or on your desk at work may help you feel more centered. Carrying a few of the treasures you find while on your adventures will help you maintain that connection. A small stone you picked up while hiking or an acorn you found while camping out can be a little lifeline to that calmer, quieter place within yourself. The pieces we connect most with are usually not the ones we buy in a shop but the random seashell we found that time on the beach.

Animals, and especially our pets, have a way of bringing the centering effects of nature to us. Bird watching, dog walking, horseback riding, or even having a fish aquarium in your home can bring you a special energy that can be both soothing and energizing at the same time. Therapy with horses and dogs has been used for years for many issues such as autism, PTSD, and severe phobias. There have been studies that show that children with learning disabilities retain more information while in the presence of animals.

One drawback is that some highly sensitive people are allergic to certain pets. If that applies to you, remember, there are hypoallergenic breeds available. Alternatively, you could buy a fish or some other allergy-friendly pet. You can also bring animal energy into your home by adding artwork.

## Water

Empaths are almost always naturally drawn to water. This is because lakes, springs, rivers, etc. help us to wash away all the unpleasant emotions that we pick up. If you are unable to get to a natural water source, even taking a bath or dancing in the rain can provide the benefit. Washing your hands is also an excellent way to make sure that someone's energy is not sticking to you when you must interact with difficult people. For maximum effect, start washing just above the wrists with plain water only; rubbing your wrists together cleanses an energy node that exists above the wrist line. This is a fast and easy solution for ridding yourself of any unwanted negative energy, in a hurry. Washing your hands is especially useful in a stressful work environment or at those dreaded family functions that so often leave us emotionally spent. Imagine that the water is gently washing the distressful energy down the drain.

When you aren't able to be near natural water, you can add water elements to your home or office instead. A small decorative fountain, seashells, a picture of the ocean, or even a recording of the sound of running water are all ways that you can invite water energy into your space without actually getting wet! More on this in the chapter "Light and Sound Vibrations".

## Epsom Salt Baths

An Epsom salt bath is another fantastic solution for dissolving any sticky emotional energy you may encounter in high-stress situations. The benefits of an Epsom salt bath are numerous, including detoxification and cleansing of your energetic and physical bodies. It raises magnesium levels, which aid with healthy rest, and reduces symptoms of depression and anxiety.

First, draw your water. You are going to need to let the salt dissolve for about fifteen minutes before you get in, so remember to adjust the temperature a little hotter than you prefer so it can cool down to perfection.

Next, add four to six cups of Epsom salt and ten to twelve drops of lavender oil (unless you suffer from migraines, in which case use cedarwood oil). The oil is completely optional, and of course, you may use any oils you like, although we particularly recommend the soothing benefits of lavender.

Let the bath "brew" and cool for the fifteen minutes or so to dissolve the salt. It is critical that you are thoroughly hydrated before beginning this bath, as it is salt's nature to draw out moisture, and it is that drawing effect we are seeking. Drink plenty of water or herbal tea while you wait. Check the temperature of the water, and give the water a good stir to dissolve any remaining salt. You can light some candles, enjoy some more tea, and soak as long as you wish.

For those who don't have access to a bathtub or simply need something a little quicker, you can dissolve one cup of Epsom salt per gallon of hot water and add five drops of the lavender or cedarwood oil. Allow five to ten minutes for brewing. You can sponge this mixture over yourself in a shower, and slowly pour it over yourself.

Lavender oil is great for releasing. Imagine the water softly running over your body and sweeping away all the stress of the day. Think of the way a gentle stream slowly carries debris downstream. As the shower water flows over you, it gently carries with it the stresses that you may have picked up from your boss, your children, your neighbors, etc.

These baths and showers can also be used for grounding or shielding by changing the oils. For grounding, use white tea oil or patchouli oil. For shielding, a combination of eucalyptus and lemon balm work well with Epsom salt's natural abilities. Imagine the water is a pure, white light filling your energetic body and then flowing outwardly.

Use these baths and showers regularly but only to a maximum of three times a week.


## Food and Exercise

These topics are discussed more fully in the chapter "Self-care." Here, under "Grounding," it is worth making a couple of points:

1.  Exercise is the best way to help you ground. Get up and get moving. You'll feel better for it! Indeed, there is one highly grounding exercise that is pleasurable on your own but is much more fun to practice together with the favorite person in your life. Ground and enjoy!

2. Heavy foods can assist with grounding, especially meat and carbo-hydrates. Rich foods such as dark chocolate can be a useful way to ground via the taste buds.

Everything in moderation, although when in doubt, exercise more and eat less!

## Grounding Summary

As with all of these exercises, find out what works for you and use it. Combine these grounding exercises with the shielding techniques from the previous chapter and the releasing processes in the next chapter. Remember, as with everything in life, it doesn't matter how good the idea is until you put it into action and keep putting it into action.

*Your beliefs become your thoughts,*
*Your thoughts become your words,*
*Your words become your actions,*
*Your actions become your habits,*
*Your habits become your values,*
*Your values become your destiny.*
— MAHATMA GANDHI

# CHAPTER 7

# Releasing

By Abbigayle and Trevor

> *The average person thinks about sixty thousand thoughts a day. This is not surprising. But it's a little disconcerting that 95 percent of the thoughts we have today are the same ones we had yesterday.*
> —DEEPAK CHOPRA

Even with all these tools in place, every one of us will find ourselves stuck in the mud from time to time. Our stuff, along with that of others, is still a reality that we all have to deal with. So what to do in the goo?

First of all, is it even yours? It's important to check in with ourselves, to make sure that what we are processing is even ours. You can do this in several ways including muscle testing, using a pendulum, asking your guides or angels, or just asking your higher self and trusting the answer you receive. (More on these techniques to come.) If it's not yours, then set the intention to release it with love and light. You can visualize sweeping the stuff from your body and rolling it into a ball. Then imagine that the ball is covered in bright healing light (this light can be whatever color you are drawn to use). Then blow the ball out into the universe like you would a dandelion, and imagine it blowing away like seeds in the wind.

## Emotion Clearing

The more we heal our own unresolved emotions, the easier it is to recognize when we are processing those of other people.

At best, emotions will flow through us in the same way that they flow through healthy children (who can have a temper tantrum one minute and be all smiles the next). As we grow older, these emotions get stuck in our physiology and color our whole outlook on life, causing us to feel stuck in outdated patterns of behavior and thought. Our brains file these emotional incidents like any other memory. Clearing those trapped emotions can help us feel lighter, happier, and in more harmony with other people around us and can remove the obstacles that interfere with living the life we were born to live.

A memory is created when proteins cause our brains cells to grow and form new connections within our mind's circuitry. These connections form a neural pathway that gets fired when the memory is recalled, and in the process, that memory becomes malleable. Scientists refer to this process as reconsolidation, and it explains why our memories can alter over time.

Reconsolidation is important because it's a point at which memory can be changed. For example, researchers in the Netherlands have worked with arachnophobes' fear of spiders. The scientist exposes someone to a tarantula, allows the person to go into a state of panic, and then gives a neural protein blocker to stop the fear from being reconsolidated. In a matter of days, the subjects were able to touch the spider without any trepidation. Their neural pathways that had associated spiders with fear had been rewired.

Although mainstream science is now determining how to clear unresolved emotions using drugs, there are many natural ways of clearing the neural pathways. Some of these are listed below:

- Emotional Freedom Technique (EFT), also known as tapping, was founded by Gary Craig in the 1990s. The user taps the end points of specific acupuncture meridians to activate the clearing mechanisms of the body. Examples of uses include limiting beliefs (e.g., rich people are bad), unresolved emotions (e.g., I feel insecure about speaking up at work), phobias, or traumas. There are plenty of free instructional texts and videos available online. Try them out. Gary Craig's official website is ww.emofree.com.

- Eye Movement Desensitization and Reprocessing (EMDR) is a psychotherapy that is commonly used to help with the symptoms of post-traumatic stress disorder (PTSD). Although EMDR can be very effective at breaking down stressful memories, it is only practiced in person by licensed therapists.

- Neuro Linguistic Programming (NLP) is a tool chest of processes for improving communication firstly with yourself and secondly with other people. It is the former category that aids in releasing trapped emotions. For instance, NLP has a renowned Fast Phobia Cure that fits well into the category of scrambling the neural pathways of old fears.

- Bradley Nelson developed his Emotion Code work around clearing trapped emotions from the protective heart wall that we create to protect ourselves from trauma.

- Trevor's system of Emotional Upgrading (partly based on Nelson's work) includes his extensive NLP background in addition to the extensive use of affirmations, to help clients heal past traumas as well as establish new strategies for living a more fulfilling life. More details at www.Thriving Empath.com.

## Journaling

Daily journaling can be a useful way of breaking the cycle of the repetitive thoughts swirling around in our heads.[1] It increases our awareness of what we are carrying around and, through that increased awareness, empowers us to choose to put down that old baggage. Journaling can help us in a number of ways:

- It releases unresolved emotions. Writing about what is bothering you can allow that "e-motion," or energy in motion, to start moving through your system again, instead of being stuck.
- It provides insights into challenging situations. Journaling can create a new perspective on a problem—for example, a relationship with a person, how you are feeling about your work, or your choice of location. New insights will open up as you give your right brain a chance to express itself in a nonlinear manner.
- It improves your health by dumping the mental noise onto paper. Better mental health translates directly into better physical health. From that quieter state of mind, your body is better able to heal itself of its dis-ease. Calm mind, calm body.

Choose any method that works for you. It could be a notebook you carry around with you, a notepad next to your bed, or a file on your computer. There are also several journaling apps available for smart devices. Journal first thing in the morning, at lunch time, or before bedtime. Aim to write for about ten to twenty minutes each day.

What do you want to write? It maybe childhood memories, nighttime dreams, current daily activities, or aspirations for the future. Get those thoughts out of your head and onto paper. You will feel better for it.

## Balancing Your Energy Cords

This visualization from the Peruvian shamanic tradition is a helpful exercise to ensure that you are using your energies wisely. To start, pick any area of your life where you want to change the energy you're investing. This can be a person or a concept—for example, a relationship, friendship, money, or job. You can do this visualization with all areas of your life. Checking all the cords within your life ensures that you have the right balance of energy with every person and field.

Next, when you have a person or concept in mind, imagine two cords connecting you to the target:

- One for energy going from you to them or the concept.
- One for energy coming from them or the concept to you.

Now, in your mind's eye, look at the two cords and ask the following:

1. Do they contain light or dark energy? If there is a dark energy present, imagine the light energy dissipating the dark until there's only light energy.
2. Is it an equal exchange of light energy? If not, are you putting out more light than you are receiving back or vice versa? Now, visualize an equal amount of light energy exchanging between the cords.
3. Do you need to increase or decrease the thickness of the cords? When you want an increase of flow, resulting in a stronger connection for a significant relationship, visualize more light energy flowing through the cords. See the cords begin to strengthen and become more vibrant.

   Maybe you want less flow? For instance, you may love your work and be passionate about it, but as a result, you're losing your perspective on your relationship with your partner. You can decrease flow to a cord when visualizing less energy flowing to and from the cord. See the cord decrease in size but still full of light. You can decrease the cords that exchange light energy with your work and increase the ones that exchange light energy with your partner.
4. Do you need to reduce the thickness on a temporary basis? Imagine the cords decreasing in light, and when you want them to increase, come back to this visualization and increase them.
5. Is it time to sever the ties completely with a particular person or concept? If so, make sure you're ready to cut them or it completely out of your life on the physical and energetic levels. If it's a person, you can imagine the cord from you to them coming back to you. Then the cord that connects the person to you going back to them. This releases the cords so you can receive your energy and the other

person receives theirs. When it's a concept like debt, sickness, jealousy, greed, or anything else you want to eliminate, imagine the cords. Now see your light detaching from the concept and coming back to you. Next, the concept's light detaching from you and going back to its origin. This detachment will have profound effects on your life.

You may want to go through all areas of your life checking the cords to ensure that you have the right balance of energy in each field and with each person.

## Cutting the Cords

Various traditions and seers talk about human consciousness being egg shaped with tendrils reaching out to everyone and everything to which we have a connection. These tendrils are called *chopi lines* in the Peruvian tradition and *aka cords* in the Hawaiian culture.

The Hawaiians have an exercise known as "cutting the aka cords." This is a multi-step process:

1. Start by using the rooting technique explained in the chapter "Grounding". Imagine that you are growing roots from your legs, going deep down into the center of the earth.
2. Visualize the cords coming out of the area of your solar plexus.
3. Use a guillotine blade to cut those cords.
4. Fire up a blow torch to a white heat to cauterize the cut ends.
5. Pack ice over those ends to cool them off.
6. Put earth over the ice to soak up the water.
7. Put armor plating over the earth to lock in your defense.
8. Then reconnect with your loved ones so as to maintain the bond.

This exercise severs any inappropriate connections that you may have created and especially the ones made by other people who have latched onto you. It also allows you to refresh your connections to friends and family, so that you can see them in the present moment rather than relating to them the way you saw them when you first made the connection.

Cord cutting is a more extreme process than Balancing Your Energy Cords in the section above. Although the Hawaiian exercise is perhaps more widely known, we suggest that you use the Peruvian technique first and save the cord cutting for extreme circumstances, in the same manner as avoiding the emergency room surgeon's knife.

## Soul Contracts

Sometimes words come out of our mouth as absolutes: always, everywhere, never, etc. When we say to someone, "I will be there for you into eternity," that is a soul-level contract that can bind you from lifetime to lifetime. Having been tortured or killed in a previous life for having practiced magic (a.k.a, for being an empath) may have resulted in a commitment of "Never again!" If you are currently tied down with an outdated vow, it can be good to break those ties.

You should use your own wording, including addressing the statement to your Higher Source. The following example is meant only as a guideline: "I wish to discontinue all soul contracts that I have ever made that no longer serve the highest good of all concerned. Please help me in disavowing these contracts, so that I am no longer under their influence and can instead align with my highest path and purpose. Thank you."

Of course, we are introducing the concept of reincarnation with this section. Think of this in the context of the quote by the statistician George Box, "All models are wrong. Some are useful." We are not asking you to believe in reincarnation, only that you consider the possibility that breaking outdated promises could be a useful strategy whether they were made in this lifetime or a past lifetime.

## Letting Go and Grieving

You can use this exercise when experiencing grief in any form: bereavement, a relationship ending, the termination of a job, or even to improve a relationship. You will need one large sheet of paper and three different color pens (one color for the circle, another for inside the cell, a third for outside the cell). The process itself is as follows:

1. With one color pen, draw a circle. This represents you.
2. Using the second color pen, write one quality you want to keep from the person or situation, and write it inside the circle. Be sure to write only one characteristic at a time; do not make a list.
3. Lock that quality inside the cell by redrawing the circle with the first color.
4. Using the third color pen, write one attribute outside the circle you do not wish to keep.
5. Lock that attribute out of the cell by drawing the circle once more using the first color.
6. Repeat this process for each element until you feel the process has been completed. You may have more qualities to let go of than you keep or vice-versa. You may keep the circle open for as many days as you need.
7. Once complete, cut out the circle with the traits you want to retain. Place this circle somewhere special and keep it. Burn the remaining paper containing those characteristics you wish to release.

We were introduced to this exercise under the title of "Tibetan Passing Away Ceremony," although we have not been able to confirm its origins.

## The Waterfall

Return to the Inner Garden that you created in the chapter "Visualization and the Power of Intent." Create a waterfall of rainbow-colored light in your garden—one that you can walk under and through. Let it cleanse your body of unwanted energies and emotions that you have picked up during your day. Place a river under the waterfall that can carry away anything that is washed off. When you are ready, step out of the waterfall, and you will be instantly dry, cleansed, and feeling lighter and more refreshed than before.

You can do this exercise anywhere, even while out shopping. Of course, if you use this process while taking a shower, the energy of the water there can help add to the imagery of washing the psychic grunge down the shower drain.

## Affirmations

What are the thought processes going on every day in your head? Worrying is creating negative affirmations for what you don't want! Be aware that every time you say to yourself, "I hope that bad event doesn't happen," the negative drops out. It is exactly like putting that request out into the universe for that very thing to take place. The same result happens if you keep worrying. "What if this bad thing happens? What if that bad thing happens?" The universe reacts by saying "I don't know why she wants such a bad thing to happen to her, but she keeps asking, so here goes!"

Affirmations are a great way to start interrupting these negative thought patterns.[2] An affirmation is a positive statement about something that you declare to be true. The mind does not distinguish between fantasy and reality, a fact that we discussed in the chapter on visualizations. Whether you are walking on a sun-soaked beach with someone you love or watching a similar scene on a movie screen, the endorphins in your body react the same way. An affirmation allows you to lock in an intention so that it can manifest in your reality.

Here are some basic guidelines for working with affirmations:

- What do you want more of in your life? Use positive affirmations around those topics, such as, I am learning how to create financial abundance.

- What do you want less of in your life? Turn those situations around into the positive qualities. For instance, if you don't like the people you are working with, you could phrase the affirmation as, I am sharing love and compassion with people at work, and I am receiving those qualities back from them.
- What emotions do you want to shift? Again, look for the opposite qualities. If you get anxious talking about money, you could phrase the affirmation as, I am confident and relaxed when discussing money.
- Start each statement with "I am." These two words activate our divinity and bring us back into right now. Our subconscious only understands the present moment.
- Phrase each affirmation in the positive. Our subconscious will drop out negative words like "not." As an example, I am not thinking about pink elephants, encourages you to immediately begin thinking about pink elephants. What is it you want to think about instead of pink elephants? If you can't find the positive alternative, replace the phrase, I am not . . . with, I am releasing. . . .
- Use incremental steps. I am a successful public speaker, may be suitable for someone who is already comfortable speaking in public, but it may not hold the necessary traction for someone who is petrified of talking in front of other people. It would be better to start with, I am comfortable speaking in front of others; I am learning to be comfortable speaking in front of others; or even, I am intending to become comfortable speaking in front of others.
- Phrasing each affirmation in multiple ways may be useful. Take the following for instance:
  - I am learning to be comfortable speaking in front of others.
  - I am safe and loved as I am learning to be comfortable speaking in front of others.
  - I am confident and courageous as I am learning to be comfortable speaking in front of others.

- I am experiencing fun and joy as I am learning to be comfortable speaking in front of others.
- I am well supported in my world as I am learning to be comfortable speaking in front of others.
- Reading the affirmations each day is good; out loud is better than silently; making eye contact with yourself in a mirror as you read them can be more effective still. Then again, due to the mind-body connection, writing the phrases out by hand may be more suitable for someone with a kinesthetic style of learning. Feel free to experiment and find the combination works best for you!
- How many times should I work with an affirmation? There are many different answers to this question. Some highly skilled facilitators will be able to work with you in such a way as to be able to create lasting change by installing an affirmation once and once only. Working on your own, you are much more likely to get the benefit by working with them every day over many weeks. How many times each day? For how many weeks? There is no right answer. Trust your intuition as to what is right for you. Try an approach, and see what different it makes.

One useful set of affirmations is "denial to clear" which we have adapted from a "stuck to clear" process in Neuro-Linguistic Programming (NLP). The principle is that we cannot move straight from a state of feeling stuck to a state of clarity; the shift has to happen in stages, and so the point is to encourage rapid movement through each stage. However, we only realize we are stuck when we move out of a state of denial, so we recommend working with the following set of affirmations:

- I am moving beyond denial.
- I am moving beyond stuck.
- I am moving beyond confused.
- I am moving beyond missing something.

- I am moving beyond being curious.
- I am clear and alert; I am aware that I know.

The bottom line on affirmations is, how do they make you feel? Worrying causes a stress reaction in our body. Our breathing gets shallow, we tense up, and all sorts of undesirable chemicals (naturally produced but nevertheless undesirable) get released into our bloodstream. When our breathing deepens, our body starts to produce all of the good endorphins that help us relax and maintain a healthy physiology. Affirmations help us release stress, as does the process of forgiveness, which we will discuss in the next chapter.

## Resources

1. **Journaling**
   *Writing to Heal: A guided journal for recovering from trauma & emotional upheaval* by James W. Pennebaker
2. **Affirmations**
   *The Game of Life and How to Play It* by Florence Scovel Shinn. First published in 1925, this is still the classic text on affirmations.

# CHAPTER 8

# Forgiveness

By Trevor

> *True forgiveness is when you can say,*
> *"Thank you for that experience."*
> —OPRAH WINFREY

- Do you want to let go of your regrets?
- Do you want to release emotional patterns triggered by the people and circumstances in your life that you often wish weren't there?
- Do you want a simple and straightforward process for creating new opportunities in your life?
- Do you want to create space for new strategies, new possibilities, and divine inspiration?

While forgiveness is essentially just another form of releasing, it is a critical one. For many people, there are times when it may seem like the most important personal technique of all. It can certainly be a life-changing experience when you start to understand what it can do for both you and the world around you.

My first lesson in forgiveness that I can remember was as an adult when my mother told me about forgiving her mother-in-law. The two of them had had a tumultuous and tense relationship. My mother said she had sat down one day and decided it was time to forgive her mother-in-law. All my mother did was repeat, "I forgive you," over and over in her head until, after some time, however long it was, she felt her chest open as her heart suddenly released years of tension in her body. Something big had shifted.

My mother was self-taught in that technique. If you read nothing else in this chapter other than that paragraph above, if you apply my mother's technique in your life, big changes will happen. The rest of this chapter is an expansion of that concept in the context of the Hawaiian art of forgiveness known as *ho'oponopono*.

Joe Vitale, in the book *Zero Limits*, writes about "a therapist in Hawaii who cured a complete ward of criminally insane patients—without ever seeing any of them. The psychologist would study an inmate's chart and then look within himself to see how he created that person's illness. As he improved himself, the patient improved." [1] The therapist was Dr. Ihaleakala Hew Len, and Dr. Len did not meet face-to-face with any of his patients. He took each inmate's file home, and as he read through the charts, he kept saying, "I'm sorry," and, "I love you," over and over again. Eventually, he healed that part of himself that had created the inmate in his life, and the patient got well. Although the traditional form is a long involved ceremony with the entire community, Dr. Len has stripped it down to this simple form of ho'oponopono.

## Responsibility

We are responsible for manifesting everything in our life. That's the bad news. The good news is that because we are responsible for creating everything in our life, it's easy to create change. I am not responsible for the pain and suffering of your life until you share it with me. At that moment, I have manifested it in my life, and I am responsible.

It is not necessary to accept this idea of being responsible for ho'oponopono to work.

Tongue-in-cheek, here's an easy route: Dump all your pain and suffering on the nearest enlightened master and let go. It's now their responsibility, and as a guru, they can deal with it! There are only two tricky steps: the first is finding the enlightened master, and the second is truly, 100 percent, letting go.

## Wording

Here's my wording of ho'oponopono:

- I'm sorry (for having created whatever it is that is disturbing me, you, and our world).
- Please forgive me (for having created it).
- Thank you (for forgiving me).
- I love you (One human being to another; I love you, me, and God just for being in my world . . . love is good!)

And so, without the commentary in parentheses, it reads: I'm sorry. Please forgive me. Thank you. I love you. Full disclosure—this is a different sequence from "I love you. I am sorry. Please forgive me. Thank you," listed in *Zero Limits*. Personally, I find, "I'm sorry. Please forgive me. Thank you. I love you," a more logical sequence, but the important thing is to find out what works for you and use it. There are various alternative forms including the shortest form, which is simply, I love you. The intent is both more important and more effective than the form.

## Forgiveness and Other People

- I forgive the people who do me wrong.
- I forgive the people who are out to get me.
- I forgive the people who (in my opinion) are complete morons.
- I forgive the people that are just taking up space in my world.

And, for sure, those negative opinions will change with the practice of ho'oponopono.

Practice:    What is it that you want to forgive other people for?
             What or who gets you hooked? Salesmen? Politicians? Telemarketers? Road rage?

It makes driving down the road a whole new experience. It can be a very different perspective to realize that the crazy people around me are there because I put them there.

Using ho'oponopono helps you avoid being sucked into another person's energy. It can free you from being "hooked" by their "stuff" and falling into the emotional trap.

You may have difficulty wanting to forgive somebody for something big. That's fine! Let it be. Begin with something small. You don't have to walk into a gym and start with the heaviest weights in the room. Work on the smaller weights first. You are building up a whole new set of muscles that you are not used to using.

You may have difficulty asking for forgiveness from others. Are you worthy of being forgiven? Can you ask forgiveness from God if not from others? Maybe the other way around, from other people if not from God?

Politicians are excellent practice material for foregiveness. By practicing on our political leaders, you get to clear yourself and the politicians, and through both you and them, you are cleansing the whole country.

Dr. Len talks about ho'oponopono as a cleansing technique. It cleans the system. For me, it has become a process: Feel some discomfort or some agitation, immediately practice foregiveness, feel better, repeat.

Eyes open or closed? My take on this is that if the thought comes up with your eyes open, practice ho'oponopono with your eyes open. It only takes three seconds! If you are lying in bed with your eyes closed and some irritation comes in, let it go by practicing with your eyes closed.

If, at this stage, you still have doubts about this work, please practice this technique on me! You can say to yourself, I'm sorry for bringing this information into my day. Please forgive me. Thank you. I love you.

Who are you saying this to? The other person, yourself, God? The answer is, yes!

## Forgiveness and Yourself

Ho'oponopono is effective for letting go of any past regrets. For me, this was the biggie! I tend to live in my head and get caught up in my thoughts, so much so that once I started, it evolved into the worst case of mental flagellation berating myself for beating myself—up until I found myself asking, "What was it again that I was beating myself up for?" This process works great as a pattern interrupter.

Practice:       What do you want to forgive yourself for?
                What have you done in the past that you wish you hadn't?
                What health challenges do you have that you prefer you
                hadn't?

If the concept of forgiving yourself doesn't work for you, try disassociating. In a disassociated state, you can go back in time to see the younger version of yourself in the situation. Reassure and forgive that younger version of yourself in the same way as you forgive others.

## Forgiveness and God

If the concept of God doesn't work for you, fill in the blank. I'm talking about the Divine, a Higher Power, the Universe, Your Higher Self, etc. Whatever works for you.

One way of thinking about ho'oponopono and God is that, because we are not separate from God, there is nothing to forgive. The original sin may well be thinking of ourselves as something separate from God. For those of us that see ourselves as being separate from God, it may be useful to ask for forgiveness from God: I'm sorry. Please forgive me. Thank you. I love you.

## Keeping Rapport

Ho'oponopono is first and foremost a personal technique. When someone is annoying you, a useful first place to go to is, internally: I'm sorry. Please forgive me. Thank you. I love you. Cleanse yourself first for creating them in your life before even thinking about correcting them.

That said, once you start noticing the changes for yourself, you may want to share the technique with your friends and family—and isn't your immediate family a perfect practice ground for foregiveness? Keep rapport!

My mother dismissed ho'oponopono on the grounds of "been there, done that." She was very much into blessings and thought nothing of standing in public places with her hand on somebody's head to bless them. However, in conversation, she could be very cynical about people and events around her. To keep rapport and still introduce her to this technique, I started to interrupt her with, "Bless them," every time she talked negatively about someone (after, of course, saying, "I'm sorry. Please forgive me. Thank you. I love you," in my head first). For her, "Bless them" worked much better.

## Practice, Practice, Practice

Have fun with this—use it! On some days, I find myself using ho'oponopono many times a day, especially on those occasions when I catch myself in the middle of an internal mental argument with myself, about someone in my life, trying to prove to myself why I'm right and they're wrong. Use it as a mantra. Share your life with it. Share your home with it. In fact, while you're at it, take a shower with it, drive your car with it, watch the news with it. Use it all the time.

Your life will be different!

## Abbigayle's Afterword on Forgiveness

Forgiveness usually doesn't happen all at once, and while ho'oponopono is a powerful tool, it may not click for everyone. That doesn't mean forgiveness is out of your reach. It simply means that like me, you may need a more proactive approach.

Try writing a letter to the person you need to forgive. (Just get everything out; you can decide whether to send it later.) In some cases, you may need to first disengage completely from that person in order to heal so that you can forgive them. If this is the case, shift your perception to something less toxic. When you begin the process, you will notice that old emotions come up. Simply release these emotions as they surface, and shift your awareness to something healthier such as meditating or taking a walk in nature. Do not try to bury these feelings, and allow yourself the time to first process and then integrate what is coming out. Remind yourself that you are no longer in that experience, and then ground yourself. Look for the positive aspects—for example, strength and understanding—you gained from what happened. Find a way to integrate those parts of that experience and release the rest, knowing it is no longer necessary for you to carry that weight.

## Resources

1. *Zero Limits: The Secret Hawaiian System for Wealth, Health, Peace, and More* by Joe Vitale and Ihaleakala Hew Len

# CHAPTER 9

# Intuition

By Abbigayle

> *Intuition is always right in at least two important*
> *ways; It is always in response to something and*
> *it always has your best interest at heart.*
> —GAVIN DE BECKER

## Intuitive Messages

How do you get intuitive messages? How do you sort out the meaningful ones from the noise? Are they voices, pictures, feelings, or knowing?

As empaths, intuition is one of the strongest gifts we are given. Unfortunately, in Western society, allowing our intuition to guide us is usually frowned upon. We are told, "Use your head!" instead of listening to our gut instinct. We hand the decision making and control to the authority figures, leaders who were themselves instructed to do as they were told, and so on. How many times have you looked back at a situation and realized if you had done what your gut told you to instead of following the crowd or doing what you were programmed to, the situation would have turned out better?

Your intuition will come to you in any number of ways. Goosebumps, more aptly named truth-bumps; tingly sensations; and shivers will tell you when you've heard the right thing or when to do or say the right thing.

Then there are the prickles on the back of your neck or the emptiness in the bottom of your gut that tells you, "Watch out, NOW!"

**Recognizing Fear**[1]

There are times when fear is valid as an intuitive warning of danger, and then there are other times when fear is entirely inappropriate. Here is a way to distinguish between the two:

- Intuitive fear, **F***** **E**verything **A**nd **R**un! is coming from the present moment.
- Habitual fear, **F**alse **E**vidence **A**ppearing **R**eal, is living in the past or future.

Intuitive fear is the tiny voice in your head that tells you "Just don't do it!" or the alarm in your entire system that warns you of danger. Your "creepy meter" goes off the charts, and everything in you is screaming to remove yourself from the situation. "This is a dangerous place to be!" or "Watch this guy; he has ill will." By listening to these intuitions and adjusting ourselves accordingly, we can save ourselves considerable grief. If you are in a situation and suddenly become fearful, take steps to protect yourself. It is better to be over-cautious and protecting yourself rather than risking harm by being too brazen. These instinctive alarms are there for a reason. Fear is an unfortunate but necessary part of our survival and also our emotional and social development. We need fear to remind us that it isn't okay to consume toxic foods or stick our hand in a burning fire. We need fear to alert us when we are at risk of harm. When we become frightened by something, we always learn from the experience and can then apply that new knowledge to future situations.

Could you be picking the fear up from somebody else? After all, you are an empath! If you are unsure, assume it's yours first and run. Ask whether it was yours afterward once you are certain you are safe.

Habitual fear lives in your mind 24/7. It keeps us living in the past or the future and stops us from experiencing the present moment. Many parents try to protect us from fear and failure, yet despite their intention, they sow unhelpful seeds of "what if" and "yes but," As adults, we have to unlearn this programming and find the difference between living in fear and living in faith.

If you find yourself living in constant fear, ask yourself "What is the pay-off?" We learn patterns of behavior when we are young, usually as survival techniques or useful strategies to keep our parents happy. The tactics that worked as children usually fail us as adults. We end up doubting ourselves before we take any chances with new relationships, new work opportunities, or any other new experiences.

In India, elephant trainers put chains around the legs of their young animals and tie the chain to a wooden stake in the ground. The baby pulls and tugs but cannot get free and eventually gives up. Years later the adult weighs several tons and could easily break the chain or rip the stake out of the ground, but it doesn't because it "knows" that it isn't strong enough. We, as humans, have also learned to accept many of our false limitations as reality. What's the voice in your head repeating to you every day? It may sound like, I'm not good enough, I don't know what I'm doing, I'm not doing enough. If you find yourself consistently hearing a particular thought in your head, playing out a repetitive behavior, or feeling an all-too-familiar emotion over the years, then that is an excellent sign that it is your own version of False Evidence Appearing Real.

Buried patterns can easily be triggered by the emotions of someone you are connected to, because you are an empath. It's easier to recognize someone else's stuff going through your system when it is unfamiliar to you. When it matches your own pattern, it is usually much harder to see. As you clear through your own garbage, it will become easier to recognize what doesn't belong to you as soon as it enters your system. When processing emotional baggage, the more you make a habit of asking, "Is this mine?" the easier it is to catch midstream.

## Intuition Development

There are many things you can do to develop your intuition. Many of the practices we mention throughout this book are keystones to channeling your inner voice and developing your intuition, such as meditation and grounding. These exercises will help you quiet the white noise drowning out your inner voice and clear your mind of anything that may block your intuitive ability.

There are several exercises you can do to strengthen your intuitive muscles.

If you have tarot or any other oracle cards, or are drawn to numbers or symbology, try picking one when you first get up. Write down your thoughts and feelings about your pick for the day. Then come back to it in the evening and jot down the important events of the day with any thoughts or feelings you remember.

You can also play a game I call On the Other Hand. Ask yourself a question. It can be about your situation; for practice, it can be a guessing-game-style question, such as, "What color is the next car going to be?" It could be something more complex, "Why do I always feel nauseous when I go to that gas station on the corner?" Write the question down with your dominant hand. Then, with your other hand, you are going to answer the question you just asked. You may find it awkward at first, and that's okay. You can think about the issue before starting to write, though when you get more comfortable, your hand will do most of the thinking for you. The reason this works is a simple matter of wiring. You will be busy using your left brain, the logical thinking part of your brain, to concentrate on writing in an unfamiliar way. This will automatically mean it won't be getting in the way of your intuitive thinking, which will be answering your question.

## Coincidences

By Trevor

There is no such thing as coincidence. As Albert Einstein said, "Coincidence is God's way of remaining anonymous." We experience messages through unexplained events much more often than we are aware. Much of the time we don't see them, or we choose to ignore them. They can take many forms: a stranger talking about exactly the right topic in front of you in line at the coffee shop, a TV broadcast that you would normally have missed, etc. I was waiting to write this section in the book when the following circumstances manifested themselves for me.

Abbey and I were discussing a client issue when, in the middle of the conversation, three woodpeckers flew outside my office window. I'd seen single woodpeckers there often, but this was the first time I had seen a family. Abbey immediately said, "Look up what woodpeckers mean."[2] I did, and the words that stood out were "there is something you have overlooked and the woodpecker it is trying to bring it back into your focus." This statement fit wonderfully into our conversation. We worked out what we had missed about the client, and we resolved the issue beautifully in a few moments.

Abbey went on to say that whenever somebody sees something new, such as an animal doing something for the first time or an unusually large gathering of a species, she always looks for its significance. So I told her about my favorite drive over the mountain to the other side of town. The first time I had driven this road, I had seen a flock of five or six wild turkeys. I had seen them in ones or twos around town before but never so many. The second time I drove this road, I saw a flock of seven or eight more. Although I had driven the road a dozen times or more since, I hadn't seen any more turkeys. Now Abbey had piqued my interest. What sign had I missed by not researching what turkeys meant all those weeks ago?

I was talking to Abbey over the phone when I turned right onto my mountain road the next day. I said, "Now that I know that those birds were probably significant, let's see if they show up today." Sure enough, a flock of seven turkeys was waiting for me on the side of the road! Furthermore, when we checked the meaning of seeing these birds, the opening lines of the description read, "It is usually a good omen indicating that great gifts are imminently forthcoming."

Given that I had gone looking for turkeys that day, and there they were, all I could say was, "Thank you!"

I continued the drive over to the friend I was visiting on the other side of the mountain. As I was driving home, I had the thought, "Suppose the Universe wanted to emphasize how much of a sign this really was. I wonder if I'll see turkeys on the way home as well."

I did! As I drove home, in a field on the side of the road, there were twenty-four wild turkeys!

## Intuition and Trust

However trusting you are, it is always good to use common sense, as illustrated in this anecdote:

There was once a spiritual man who had lived a good life. So much so that God came to him and told him "If you ever need my help, I will save you." One day, the local river flooded over the banks and submerged the whole town under water. Pete was forced to climb onto his porch roof. While he was sitting there, a man in a boat came along and told Pete to get in with him.

Pete said, "No, that's okay. God will take care of me." So off rowed the man in the boat.

The water rose higher, so Pete climbed onto his roof. Another boat came along, and this person, too, offered to take Pete to safety.

Pete replied, "No, that's okay. God will take care of me." So once more, the person in the boat left.

The water continued to rise. Pete climbed onto his chimney, and a helicopter came along. A woman lowered a rope ladder for him and told Pete to climb to safety.

Pete said, "That's okay. God will take care of me."

Finally, the water rose over the whole house, and Pete drowned. When Pete got to heaven, he met with God and said, "I thought you were going to take care of me! What went wrong?"

God responded, "I sent two boats and a helicopter. What's your problem?"

## Resources

1. **Recognizing Fear**
   *The Gift of Fear: Survival Signals That Protect Us from Violence* by Gavin De Becker
   *Feel the Fear . . . and Do It Anyway* by Susan Jeffers

2. **Coincidences and Animals**
   Spirit Animal Totems and their messages: www.spirit-animals.com
   *Animal-Speak: The Spiritual & Magical Powers of Creatures Great & Small* by Ted Andrews

# CHAPTER 10

# Intuitive Tools

By Trevor

> *We are symbols, and inhabit symbols.*
> —RALPH WALDO EMERSON

## What Are Intuitive Tools?

This chapter discusses divination tools including tarot cards, pendulum dowsing, muscle testing, and others that help us to tap into our intuition. In an ideal world, we wouldn't need these techniques. Our intuition would be strong enough to give us all the information we need, without these tools. But in that ideal world, our telepathic abilities would be such that we wouldn't need telephones: we could spontaneously relocate, so we wouldn't need cars; and our inner sense of direction would always tell us where to go instead of using navigation devices.

We are a long way from living in that world! As empaths, we are moving in that direction. There are few people around who can download information sufficiently well that they have a clear line of communication, but most of us need a lot of help. Like someone who has hurt their leg, it is useful to use a crutch for a while. You don't want to use it forever—only for as long as it takes to strengthen your body. Similarly, using these tools will enhance your intuition along the way. It is best to listen more and more to your intuition as it develops rather than depending too much on these tools.

These techniques work because they allow us, as we use them, to bypass the logic of our left brain and tap into the right-brain knowingness of our bodies. The left brain will analyze, judge, intellectualize, and lie—and provide us with an entirely justifiable reason for giving us misinformation. The right brain doesn't lie. Our body doesn't lie—more on that soon. When we tap into that right-brain wisdom, we can get answers that help us live a life that is more aligned with our true nature. The symbolism of many of the intuitive tools that we discuss below speaks in a language that the right brain understands well.

Are these divination tools unscientific? Of course, but everything that empaths know to be true—picking up energies and emotions from other people—is beyond the capabilities of modern science to prove. If you are going to use any of these intuitive tools, just remember, the mainstream world doesn't know what you are doing. What they don't know about, they won't mock you for. Be judiciously discreet.

## Using These Tools Yourself

The first advantage of using any of these tools yourself is that as you use them, your intuitive muscles will grow by leaps and bounds. Secondly, you can trust your own intentions when you are doing your own reading; you know you have your own your best interests at heart in a way that may not be true for any other person who might be doing a consultation for you.

The flip side is that you can influence the reading by misinterpreting the answer to be what you expect it to be. As an example, in my younger days, I had just started dating a new girlfriend, and I used one of these oracles to inquire about the relationship. The answer came back very clearly talking about marriage in a way that surprised me, but, hey, I could be open for that. A week later, she announced to me that she was indeed getting married—to somebody else, who I had no idea about! When I reviewed the reading that the oracle had given me, all the signs were there, but I had chosen to ignore fundamental aspects. This type of misinterpretation is what can happen when you are emotionally involved in your own reading.

On the other hand, what can happen if you use somebody else as your reader? In every profession, there are skilled people and there are those who are unskilled. There are people in the world who, in general, will look after your best interests. There are also plenty who will take advantage of you. The same rule applies specifically to psychics, intuitives, and healers. Ideally, you want to find the skilled intuitive who puts your welfare first.

Primarily, be cautious. If you use any manner of commercial psychic you may get quality information in the initial session, you may not. Trust your intuition. They may start telling you that only they can help you with the things they see for you. They may drop hints that they and they alone are privy to some secret information about you. At this point, get ready to run because the next line will be some variation of "Pay me lots of money and I can help you!" It's a scam, and they are about to turn you into a victim. The more their seeds of doubt are rattling around in your head, the more you are hooked, and they are about to reel you in.

## Asking the Right Question

The most important part of using any divination tool is asking the right question. It goes with the territory that, to ask the best question, we need to be able to be specific about what we are looking for. Consider the analogy of asking, "What is the difference between red and blue?" versus "What is the difference between the red spectrum of light and the blue spectrum of light?" The first question allows for many subjective answers. The second restricts the answer to a more objective range; for example, a 650-nanometer wavelength for red and 475 nanometers for blue.

So here are some pointers for asking the right questions:

- Treat the process of asking as if you were sitting in front of a wise old sage who, with much patience, is willing to help with your issues. Do your homework ahead of time to ensure you are using the best possible phraseology. Be respectful of the process.

- Focus on a single question. Ideally, write it out, speak it out loud, or both. If you have multiple questions running round your head, the answers will be as confused as your thinking.

- Look for hidden assumptions in your questioning. If your soul purpose is to be an artist, it might be worthwhile to stop asking which banking job is the right one for you.

- Ask only questions about yourself, not other people. However, you can ask about them if you have their permission. Otherwise, it is an invasion of their privacy to ask about them. Also, the other person has free will and can choose a different path. The answer you get may be the one that is most appropriate for YOU to receive, which may not be a correct reflection of an accurate answer.

- Start by asking, "Is it appropriate for me to ask [this question]?" This checks whether or not we are even asking the right question for the circumstances.

- Do you keep asking variations of the same question? Be sure to check yourself as to whether you are unwilling to accept the answers you have already been given. A close friend or mentor may be able to reflect back to you what you are resisting.

- "Is it for the highest good of all concerned that . . ." is probably the most potent way to begin these power questions.

- Ask about health and spiritual well-being rather than material concerns. You can ask, "Is it for the highest good of all concerned for me to commit to this business endeavor?" The answer may be yes, but that doesn't necessarily mean that the business venture will be successful for you. It may just mean that you are going to learn some valuable lessons the hard way. Many of us have, in our folly, tried to use divination as a way to get rich quickly. I was one of those fools in my younger days! Usually, the answers are good enough, for long enough, to get us used to trusting the process just a little too much. The result is falling back to Earth with a pretty hard bump. Do yourself a favor and avoid that mistake!

- Be careful about your choice of words. Asking, "Can I ...?" will always get a yes unless you are asking if you can defy the laws of physics. If you are asking, "Will I ...?" be aware that the future holds many possibilities; are you really asking about the likelihood of something happening? Most of the time asking if something is for the highest good of all concerned provides a useful guide.
- Be as precise as possible. For example, "Is it for the highest good of all concerned for me to trust my team at work?" may provide a no, simply because of one person in that group. Asking about specific team members will be more revealing.
- If you can discuss your question with a good friend or coach first, so much the better. A good practitioner will often go through a line of discussion with you that may significantly change your approach.
- Remember that whatever the question, the answer is coming from bypassing your conscious mind to access the subconscious or higher self. However, the answer will reflect your thoughts and desires if you don't quiet your mind first.

## Getting Accurate Answers

All of these intuitive tools tap into your body's natural wisdom in one form or another. The "Energetic Corrections" section in the chapter "Self-Care" provide three things (grounding, drinking water, and tapping your thymus gland) that are very useful in ensuring the best possible results. These energetic corrections are especially appropriate for both muscle testing and for dowsing with a pendulum, which heavily rely on you being centered in your body.

Just as it is good to discuss your question with a good friend or coach, it is equally beneficial to discuss the answers with someone. Getting the right answers is one thing; understanding them is another. Some of the best answers you will ever get will only be obvious with the advantage of 20/20 hindsight.

## How Do You Feel About a Coin Toss?

Flipping a coin as a means of divination is probably as old as coins themselves. It is certainly the easiest tool for getting a yes or no answer, but its real value is less about the result of the toss and more about how you feel about the result. In that first second when you see the coin land, you may get a happy "Yes!" reaction in your body or a heavy "Oh no! Let's try best of three instead." At that moment, you know which answer your ego wanted. As to whether or not you then have the trust to accept the answer you were given is up to you.

## Abbigayle's Decision Rock

When I was a child, I often found making even the simplest of decisions to be difficult. Milk or juice? Nuggets or burgers? I would feel my heart start racing, and my hands would start sweating. My brain would freeze, and I would be stuck standing there staring blankly.

One day when I was maybe seven or eight years old, someone I knew only as "Mr. Rock Man" gave me a small black stone with a spot on one side. He told me that it was a magic "decision rock" and that it would help me decide anything I ever needed to. All of a sudden, my life was simplified. I used my stone to select everything from my lunch choices to the "important" things like which science project to choose and even with which parent I would spend holidays or birthday. In hindsight, I see that usually, I would put the "good" or "right" (meaning the one I was subconsciously drawn to) answer on the white side. And if it didn't land on the white, I would find myself coming up with reasons for a do-over. I would tell myself, "It bumped my foot, so that didn't count," close my eyes, and try again. Sure enough, my rock would fall to the floor, and when I opened my eyes, the answer I wanted was right in front of me. I fully trusted that stone to tell me exactly what I needed to know, and it did just that 100 percent of the time. It did because I *believed* that it did. It was no coincidence that the stone I was given was what I now know to be snowflake obsidian, a stone that is deeply connected to inner truth and intuitive wisdom. By subconsciously planting the seed of intention, Mr. Rock Man had helped me connect with my inner voice, by giving me my very first intuitive tool in the form of a "magic" rock.

## Muscle Testing[1]

"Is what I am experiencing mine?" is one of the most important questions you can ask as an empath. Muscle testing and, in the next section, pendulum dowsing are two excellent tools to help answer that question.

We said at the top of this chapter that the body can't lie and that only the mind knows how to lie. When we tap into the natural intelligence of the body, we can bypass the mind and get more accurate information from the physical body than we can from the mental one. There are now many derivative forms of muscle testing under a variety of names, although *applied kinesiology* is one of the more established modes.

The way this can work, for illustration, is that the client will hold their arm out to the side, parallel to the floor. The practitioner will ask a question such as "Does this person need a particular nutritional supplement?" while gently pushing down on the arm. The arm muscles will go weak for a no and hold strong for a yes.

It is possible to self muscle test. It takes time to master and is most useful for a limited number of questions. It is challenging to learn to keep the intellect out of the way and fully trust what your body is telling you.

The easiest way to get a sense of self muscle testing is with the following procedure:

1. Stand in flat shoes or barefoot with your feet shoulder width apart.
2. Close your eyes. Take a few deep breaths. Ensure that you are centered and quiet inside.
3. Think of a particular question that you want to ask. Two good ones for testing purposes can be the following:
   - "Is artificial sugar beneficial for my physical body?" The answer is an almost universal no.
   - "Is artificial sugar detrimental for my physical body?" The answer is an almost universal yes.
4. After a few moments, you will become aware of being gently drawn forward or pushed backward. Forward is an attraction, a yes; backward, a no. A few people may calibrate differently; for example, a yes may pull to the left, a no to the right. Determine what works for you and adjust accordingly.

If you don't get a clear response, try the following:

- Make sure you are fully centered.
- Drink a glass of water to ensure you are hydrated.
- Set the intention that you will get a distinct response for a yes or no answer.

The sway test is the easiest method to learn for self-muscle testing, but there are other ways. One of these is to join thumb and forefinger on each hand as two interlocking circles. As you pull your hands apart, your fingers will stay locked for a yes or be weak, breaking apart, for a no. The challenge here is to set your intention such that you easily hold your fingers at the right firmness to give you a definitive yes or no.

## Pendulums and Dowsing

A pendulum is a small weight suspended on the end of a chain or thread, which is held in your hand. You can purchase one ready-made or make your own. It can be as basic as a key or a ring on the end of an eight- to twelve-inch string, or it can be as sophisticated as you want it to be. As you become more experienced using different pendulums, you are sure to develop a feel for your favorite one.

To get started, hold the string in your hand with the weight dangling down. You can support your elbow on a flat surface or simply tuck it into your body; determine what arm position feels right for you. Initially, you will want the pendulum to show you how it wants to give you a yes and a no. You can ask out loud or silently; it makes no difference as long as your speech and your thoughts are aligned. If you are saying one thing and thinking another, your answers will be confused. The pendulum may move back and forth, side to side, clockwise, or counterclockwise. The direction doesn't matter as long as you get a calibration that works for you.

Some people like to set a calibration for some or all of the following answers: absolutely yes, absolutely no, sort of, can't say, or ask later. Some people find it easier to have the answers written out on a piece of paper. As you focus your eyes or move your pendulum over a particular answer on the sheet, watch how the pendulum reacts to each choice. When you are first starting out, it may take several minutes to get unambiguous movements.

Once you have calibrated how your subconscious wishes to work with the pendulum, you are ready to start asking questions—specifically, questions to which the answer is expected to be a straight yes or no.

## Tarot, Oracle Cards, and the *I Ching*

Muscle testing and pendulums are great for closed-end questions to which you can expect a yes or no answer. Tarot cards and other divination tools are better at answering open-ended questions. With these tools, it is better to ask, "What do I need to know about [*name your topic*]?" Be as specific as you can about that one topic.

Tarot card decks have been around since the 1400s and were initially used more as playing cards than as divination tools. The traditional decks contain the *major arcana*, a set of twenty-two cards of archetypal images that include, for example, the Fool, the Magician, the High Priestess, the Empress, and the Emperor. The manual shuffling and dealing of the deck allow for the human psyche to select the appropriate cards and provide a reading based on traditional interpretations. These deep-rooted symbols often speak directly to our unconscious mind although it can sometimes be a challenge to translate the symbolism into relevance for our daily lives.

The *I Ching* is a two-thousand-year-old Chinese oracle known in the West primarily through Richard Wilhelm's German translation, which was rendered into English by Cary F. Baynes.[2] The *I Ching* is consulted traditionally by casting fifty yarrow stalks, although using three coins is the more modern and much easier method. The psychologist and mystic Carl Jung was intrigued by the *I Ching* and wrote the introduction to Wilheim's translation. Many modernized adaptations have been written, as the traditional text can seem esoteric and obtuse at times but can be but very rewarding if you are willing to put in the effort. The *I Ching* was my oracle of choice when I inquired about my girlfriend in the story at the beginning of this chapter.

In recent years, many non-traditional oracle card decks have come on the market, including fairy cards, angel cards, animal cards, etc. There is nothing inherently better or worse about these decks. As with all forms of divination, the most important aspect is not about the tool but how well the practitioner can interpret the results that the oracle provides. As with all the tools presented here, you will find that you resonate more with some than others. Again, find what works for you.

## Astrology[3]

If you know your time and place of birth, it can be fascinating to get a professional reading—especially if you can get a recommendation to an expert. Let's face it; there is a vast difference between a generalized horoscope, "twelve sizes fit all," and a professional astrological reading that is personalized for you.

A quality reading is less about immutable predictions and more about potentials and opportunities. In particular, the type of work that is referred to as *transformative astrology* maps our character and is oriented toward maximizing personal growth. It uses patterns, such as the seasons and movements of planets, to help us understand the direction of our lives.

Astrology is a self-awareness tool.

Transformative astrology assumes that each of us came here for a purpose. Using a holistic system of symbols, it explores the character tools we have for whoever we came here to be—including how that character integrates into larger communities and the world.

True to the founders of humanistic astrology, philosopher Dane Rudhyar and psychologist Carl Jung, transformative astrology is not fatalistic. Planets are not causes of anything; they are merely symbols for larger processes. Neither our characters nor our futures are fated or fixed. In fact, awareness of our character through astrological self-reflection expands our sense of identity. It helps us to be who we are and by doing so, discover our own destinies.

For this reason, a transformative astrological consultant does not tell clients what to do. He or she does not dictate choices or make absolute predictions; rather, the consultant's job is to hold up a mirror to help clients explore their potential, especially as culture transformers.

There are three common types of readings:

1. Your unique birth chart – Natal charts reflect the sky at the exact moment we are born. Our general talents, abilities, goals, and challenges can be seen in these charts. This is where people usually begin their astrological journey.

2. Trends and life passages – Astrology offers many methods for exploring ongoing personal development:
   - *Transits* indicate how we experience collective processes—what is going on "out there." Instead of making predictions ("you'll meet a tall, dark stranger"), transformative astrology suggests how our energies—professional, creative, or romantic—may be reflected in everyday life. Transits focus on how our character develops through time and often take into account larger historical trends. They help us strategize around our everyday life processes.
   - *Progressions* map inner and personal processes—what is going on "in here."
   - Progressions show us how we may use our inner energies to flow with our outer life's rhythms.
   - *Solar returns*, which occur every year around birthdays, outline themes for the coming year.
3. Relationships – Of course, we do not exist in isolation. Astrology has millennia of experience to help us understand the dynamics of relationships—how we interact with parents, children, siblings, friends, bosses, coworkers, and romantic partners.
   - *Synastry* spells out how we see another person: where we get along and how to grow through challenges that arise.
   - *Composites* give a picture of the relationship as a whole—how two charts give rise to a third, which symbolizes the unique relationship between the two people involved.

## Numerology

*Numerology* is the practice of using numbers as a predictive oracle. It can be as simple as assigning significance to specific numbers, such as lucky seven or unlucky thirteen. In its more complex forms, it can include assigning numerical values to the letters in your name or adding up the numbers in your birthday. It can take the time and date that you ask a question and use those in conjunction with your name and date of birth to provide an answer. The numbers extracted out of such a formula can then be ascribed a meaning.

We talked about coincidences in the chapter "Intuition". Some people choose to assign significance when a particular number is seen multiple times during the day. Repetitive numbers, especially 11:11, are particularly popular in this respect. These are often referred to as *angel numbers*.[4]

Neither Abbigayle nor I feel strongly toward numerology, so this section was included to acknowledge it for those who do. Personally, the following story illustrates any bias I have about numeric coincidences.

In the book *Golf in the Kingdom*, the author, Michael Murphy, refers to his experience on the golf course when he repeatedly heard in his head, "You are not lined up straight. Line up again." Eventually, he realized that the voice wasn't talking about the angle of his putter but rather the fact that his life wasn't lined up straight. He was living the life of a workaholic, even sleeping in his office, and the only time he slowed down enough to listen to his inner guidance was on the golf course.

When I first heard Murphy's story of not being lined up straight, I thought it would be nice to have a way to be reminded when we are lined up straight in our lives. I had the thought, let it go, and forgot about it. This was back in the late 1980s. It must have been a few weeks later when I started to notice strange coincidences. Frequently, I would glance at my digital watch, and the number of seconds would match the number of minutes. Particularly noticeable was when the hour matched the minutes matched the seconds as in 4:44:44 or 5:55:55. These coincidences went on for weeks. The weeks turned into months, and the months turned into years. I stopped wearing a digital watch, but the same pattern continued with the hours and minutes on digital clocks.

Michael Murphy's story remained a favorite of mine, and eventually, after some years, I finally remembered that quiet thought, "Wouldn't it be nice to have a way of being reminded that we are lined up straight in our lives." It finally occurred to me that I had created my own system, and the digital coincidences were my reminders that I was lined up straight. Once I had that realization, the number of times that the clocks lined up for me went back to a much more regular frequency.

Coincidences do occur. They almost always have significance, if you are open to finding the meaning. However, the importance for you may be different from that for the next person.

## Ouija Boards

This section is included only as firm advice for an intuitive tool to avoid. Ouija boards are sold in toy shops as a device for communicating with spirits or other disembodied entities, whatever you prefer to call them. It is a flat board on which are written the alphabet, numbers zero through nine, and the words *yes* and *no*. It is intended to be used by a few people each placing a finger on the planchette, or pointer; the assumption being that a spirit may spell out messages without the participants consciously moving the pointer.

We mention Ouija boards here because empaths, especially those of you of the younger generations, may get invited to use one just because you are tempted to explore all your gifts—although mediumship is not directly related to being an empath. It may sound harmless, and it could be a powerful tool in the right hands, but it can invite all sorts of disembodied entities into your space. It is like leaving your doors and windows wide open all night in the wrong part of town; you might be okay, but why take the risk? Ouija boards should only be used be somebody who is skilled in working in this area, and someone skilled in this area doesn't need a Ouija board. Please leave this particular tool well alone.

## Other Forms

There are many other types of oracles: tea leaves, crystal balls, and palmistry to name but a few. There are people calling themselves psychic readers, clairvoyants, channelers, mediums, and many other names. Most of the indigenous cultures have their own traditional forms. The practitioner is much more important than the tool.

If you use any of the recommended oracles in this chapter, they will help you develop your intuition. Having other people use them on your behalf will give you information and guidance, if they are genuine. Having scam artists pretend to give you readings will do nothing but hurt your head, your heart, and your wallet. It can be fun and beneficial to swim in these waters, but beware of the sharks!

## Resources

1. **Muscle Testing**
   *Your Body Doesn't Lie: Unlock the Power of Your Natural Energy!* by Dr. John Diamond
2. **I Ching**
   *The I Ching or Book of Changes* by Richard Wilhelm and Cary F. Baynes
3. **Astrology**
   There are many good introductions to astrology, although Kim Rogers Gallagher's *Astrology for the Light Side of the Brain* is the most entertaining.
   Linda Goodman's 1968 book, *Linda Goodman's Sun Signs*, popularized the subject for many people.
   Stephen Arroyo's *Astrology, Karma & Transformation: The Inner Dimensions of the Birth Chart* (along with all of Dane Rudhyar's books) most resemble the approach of our favorite transformative astrologer, Chris Largent, who can be reached at ideahse@aol.com.
4. **Angel numbers**
   *Angel Numbers 101* by Doreen Virtue.
   See also: http://sacredscribesangelnumbers.blogspot.com

# CHAPTER 11

# Self-care

By Trevor

> *When you take time to replenish your spirit, it*
> *allows you to serve others from the overflow.*
> *You cannot serve from an empty vessel.*
> —ELEANOR BROWNN

## The Mind-Body Connection

Your emotions impact your physiology, and your body will reflect back your emotions. A particular emotional pattern will have an effect on a limited number of areas of your body. If you want to know what you were thinking and feeling last year, look at your body now. If you want to know what your body will be like next year, look at your thoughts now. As Caroline Myss puts it in *Anatomy of the Spirit*, "All our thoughts, regardless of their content, first enter our systems as energy. Those that carry emotional, mental, psychological, or spiritual energy produce biological responses that are then stored in our cellular memory. In this way, our biographies are woven into our biological systems, gradually, slowly, every day." [1]

When Myss first started working as a medical intuitive, she quickly started to realize that people with the same illness had similar emotional issues. As she says in *The Creation of Health*, "Every illness or dysfunction a person develops is an indication of a specific type of emotional, psychological, or spiritual stress. Each of the characteristics of an illness, such as its location in the physical body, is symbolically important."[2]

Louise Hay pioneered the use of affirmations as antidotes for the impact of emotional distress on the body. As one simple example, in *You Can Heal Your Life*, Hay says that breath "represents the ability to take in life" and provides the affirmation "I love life" as an antidote to problems with breathing.[3]

Tribal shamans have always passed down knowledge of this mind-body connection and have used this understanding for their healing practices. Western science is catching up as Dr. Candace Pert has shown in her leading work as a neurobiologist.[4] She has shown that neuropeptides, chemical signals in the body, are the physical representation of emotions.

The point here for the empath is that your physical body is not an accident of nature. It reflects a state of mind, and if you can change your thoughts, you can change your body. Furthermore, the emotions you pick up from the people around you will impact your body, unless you keep your energetic system clear. The self-care tools presented here and throughout the book can help you with that process.

## Five Steps for Self-care

1. Trust your instincts. If it feels wrong, don't do it. If it feels right, go for it.
2. Speak from your heart!
   - Speak the sweet truth.
   - Say it lovingly, say it compassionately, but say it!
   - Say no when appropriate to protect your boundaries and avoid taking on more than your system can handle. As empaths, we tolerate way too much for way too long to try to keep other people happy. Intolerance has its place, too.

- Say yes, when appropriate, if that is what will make you feel good (especially if it stretches your personal envelope a little bit). Keep saying yes to your passion. What can you do every day or every week to keep your dreams alive and move just a tiny step closer to them?
- Let go of the need to keep other people happy.
- Speak well of yourself—to others and especially to yourself.

3. Let go of what you can't control.
4. Avoid drama and negativity.
5. Live with kindness, love, and compassion—for other people and yourself.

## Energetic Corrections

The following are three quick checks to make sure your energy is flowing the way it should:

1. Ground yourself. Take a few moments to reconnect with the earth. Imagine that you are growing roots from your legs, through the soles of your feet, deep down into the center of the earth. This exercise is the rooting technique explained in the chapter on grounding.
2. Drink a glass of water. Many of us spend most of our days dehydrated, and our sensory system can be so weak that thirst may be mistaken for hunger. Increasing the amount of water in our system will help the nurture the body, especially during the summer months. When you are rehydrated, you should notice a significant shift in your energy levels within just a few minutes.
3. Tap your thymus gland for about twenty seconds. To start, find your thymus gland by locating your collarbone, and position your finger on its end, near the hollow at the center of your neck. Keeping your finger to just one side of center, slide your finger down about two inches to the spot just below your second upper rib. You should be

about halfway between your collarbone and your heart. Tap that area for thirty seconds to one minute to stimulate life back into your thymus gland. If you need a hint as to why this is important, the Greek word *thymos* means "life energy" or "passion"!

## Zipping

This is a great process adapted from Donna Eden, that offers you more confidence, positivity, centeredness, mental clarity, and shielding from negative energies around you.[5]

1. Start by getting your energy flowing. You can do this by simply clapping or rubbing your hands together. Better still, tap your thymus for about twenty seconds (see the instructions above in the section "Energy Corrections").
2. Place one or both of your hands, palms facing inward, just in front of your pubic bone.
3. Inhale deeply as you slowly move your hand straight up the center line of your body, zipping up toward your lower lip. Imagine locking this line closed as your reach your mouth.
4. Repeat steps 1 and 2, three times.

While doing this, you can use affirmations such as, "I am confident, positive and centered." The process will increase the power of the affirmations.

You can practice zipping as often as you wish. Especially use anytime you are going into any social situation you find challenging.

## Food and Exercise

There is a vast quantity of mainstream literature on the topics of food and exercise, and they are crucial components of self-care for the empath. The mainstream, of course, doesn't tailor their advice for empaths and other highly sensitive people. Above all else, if your diet and exercise regime is not working for you—you are not following it or you don't feel well on it—it doesn't matter how many experts agree on how good it should be for you. And for every expert who says it is right, there are plenty more who are sure to be advising something different. Listen to your body. Follow your instincts.

That said, we hope the following paragraphs help you to gain a different perspective on the mainstream literature on these topics.

## Food

Many sensitive people put on weight as a form of protection. Extra body weight helps to ground and, in grounding, provides some shielding against the barrage of emotions from other people. That's not right or wrong, a judgement or criticism; it is merely an observation. By using some of the other tools in this book to provide help with grounding and shielding, you will find alternatives to using eating as a means of protection.

Our bodies absorb nutrition best when we are feeling happy and relaxed and are eating slowly. This is wisdom that ayurveda, the ancient Indian medical discipline, has understood for centuries and which modern science is just starting to catch up with. Eating what you enjoy and enjoying what you eat is a great place to start. Allow yourself the chance to make changes slowly. If you need to cut out sodas, for instance, it can be much easier to cut gradually down over a period of days or weeks rather than going cold turkey immediately. However, if you are the type of person who does everything "whole hog" or not at all, then you know what works for you, so go for it!

If you are going to try dietary cleanses, do so in moderation. There is evidence to suggest that long fasts, two weeks or more, may do more harm than good over the long term. Just a three day cleanse can be a great way to reset the taste buds to help make a long-term change.

**Exercise**

What is the best exercise program? The one that you are prepared to keep doing on a regular basis. If you are enjoying the activity, you will keep doing it. If you don't enjoy it, chances are you'll stop.

The objective of an exercise program for empaths is to get you back into your body and to keep you connected to the earth. Of course, all the usual health considerations are important, and if you have any physical concerns, please discuss any new exercise regime with your doctor.

Grounding doesn't need a full cardiovascular workout, but you do have to be moving. If you are living a sedentary lifestyle, the energy you are picking up from other people is much more likely to get stuck in your body. So if you are not living an active lifestyle, find something, anything, that gets you out of the chair. Yoga, tai chi, stretching, walking, dancing, swimming, cycling. What is going to get you moving? Is listening to music going to help you to exercise? What about podcasts or audiobooks? The goal is to make sure you look forward to the experience.

The most important muscle is the mind! The first twenty-one days of a new program are less about working out the body than about getting into the habit of exercising. Don't push your body so hard at first that you are going to be sore. That is just going to associate the pain with working out, and your mind will find excuses to avoid the pain. If you take the first three weeks easy, you will be settling your mind into the habit so that by the fourth week, your body will be starting to feel like it's ready to be pushed a little more.

## The Five Tibetan Rites

The Five Tibetan Rites are an off-mainstream set of exercises, but they are a gentle, holistic way of getting your body moving.[6] They were first publicized by Peter Kelder in a 1939 publication titled *The Eye of Revelation* and more recently popularized under the title *Ancient Secret of the Fountain of Youth*.

That title itself introduces the somewhat extreme claims for the effectiveness of the exercises. Nevertheless, they are a compact set of movements that take only ten minutes a day, and as we have said above, any exercise that you commit to doing is infinitely better than any exercise that you are not doing!

Rather than duplicate the exercises here, we recommend you buy Kelder's book or research the rites online at Wikipedia.org or Youtube.com.

## Mind-Heart-Gut Exercise

We are brought up in the West to listen to our heads, not to our heart or our gut. As empaths, our goal is to listen to our intuition, and this exercise encourages that process:

1. Visualize energy coming up from your intestines, up your back, and connecting with your brain at the brain stem at the top of your spine.
2. Let that energy flow into the whole of your brain, allowing all the knowledge and wisdom of your gut and heart to seep into your mental awareness.
3. Allow the knowledge in your head to flow down the front of your body, to your chest and on into your digestive system.
4. Keep that flow going for a few minutes, allowing your body's intelligence centers—mind, heart, and gut—to communicate with each other.
5. Repeat daily.

You may feel an energy shift during this exercise as you open up new lines of communication. New intuitive insights may open up during your daily activities that don't seem to have any logical justification. Whatever happens, trust that you are doing the process correctly and just be aware of possible changes taking place for you.

## Coaching

There are many types of coaches available. General life coaches, relationship coaches, business coaches, and the authors, of course, as empath coaches, among many others. Why? Because we weren't meant to go through life on our own. Evolution developed us to thrive in a village where the village elders would have served as our coaches. In today's world, we have to go out and find our sage advisors for ourselves.

We can see other people's baggage so much more clearly than we can see our own. A good coach can help you move past your blocks and progress faster toward whatever it is you are working on than you can on your own.

Weekend joggers don't hire coaches; top-performing athletes do! If you want to be a peak performer, find yourself a coach.

## Creativity and Art

Any form of artistic creativity encourages right brain thinking, and this, in turn, nurtures your intuition. Using any form of art is going to help develop your empathic abilities. Don't set your sights on producing a masterpiece. Judgments about what is good or bad only hinder the creativity, so let all of that go and just allow the flow. In fact, the more you can be in the mindset of a beginner, the better. If you are already skilled in a particular art form, then pick up a new one. Have you always wanted to dance or act? Even if you think you can't carry a tune, buy a cheap musical instrument and play around. Painting or drawing, it's not about the outcome; it's about feeding your right brain.

### Trevor's Story

As a child, I played logic games and mathematical puzzles for fun. It was a natural extension of my left-brain abilities that I went on to make myself a career in Information Technology. When I started my twice-daily practice of meditation, that began to change. My aunt bought me a medieval psaltery, a triangular, harp-like instrument played with a bow, for my birthday. My unspoken thought was, "Why would you give me this? Don't you know I am tone deaf?" I played with it for a little while and soon realized that I could pick out "Three Blind Mice" by ear. Yes, I was in my mid-twenties; it was still an accomplishment for me. I never got anywhere close to a standard that you could call good, but I had fun for a few months. I did something similar with Betty Edward's book *Drawing on the Right Side of the Brain*, which has remarkable success at teaching complete beginners to draw.[7] I picked up this book in my fifties after hearing Daniel Pink talking about the importance of right-brain creativity in an interview with Oprah Winfrey. My drawing skills did increase although, again, I only practiced for a few months. One of the philosophical lessons I learned in that process was how much drawing is about seeing what is actually in front of you rather than what you THINK is there. How much in life are we reacting to what we believe is there, because of our programming, rather than what is really there?

## Abbigayle's Story

I never considered myself a creative type. If you had asked me when I was younger, I would have told you with 100 percent confidence, "I suck at art." I would have told you this standing backstage of my fifth dance recital for that year or while I was in the middle of writing some fantastical story about the tree people and how they decided to go underground eons ago to hide from the dinosaurs. My problem wasn't that I was "no good at artsy stuff" like I told myself, it was that I didn't understand what true creativity was. It would be years before I could look back on those things and see how truly creative of a child I was. Now I can see that I was frustrated by the boundaries of perfectionism. In fact, I distinctly remember failing art class because I couldn't stay within the confines of the assignment. I guess my art teacher had never heard of abstract before. I remember thinking that there were too many rules for me to be artistic. Recognizing that there are no rules in art was the most liberating thing I ever learned. Suddenly it made sense to me: I wasn't the one who was no good at art; I was just the one with art that others didn't understand yet. What's more, it wasn't made for them to understand; it was mine and mine alone. I was free to put whatever in or take out as I needed to express my whole truth.

Over the years, I have had many creative outlets. Dance was my first love; I still find myself getting lost in the rhythm of a random song playing, and my body just begins to move along. Later, I began to write poetry, short stories, and eventually started writing for the school newspaper. I've done jigsaw puzzles for hours, latch hook, and spin art. I've made thousands of beaded bracelets for friends and family and even tried my hand at origami, which I quickly learned I did not have the dexterity for.

I've also found my creativity outside of what others might consider to be traditional outlets. Cooking for example, is one of my cathartic creative outlets. There's just something about the process of creating a wonderful meal and enjoying the fruits of that process in such a complete way, that is to me both grounding and uplifting simultaneously.

Science is yet another example of creativity outside the box. They say that necessity is the mother of all invention; I say that creativity is. It's all fine and well to need something, but until someone takes it upon themselves to create it, you're just going to go on needing. Inventors and scientists have been working to fill this necessity for centuries. It is thanks to the creative minds like Albert Einstein, Thomas Edison, and Leonardo da Vinci that the world is what it is today. We can take a page from their books and experiment with the world around us, explore it, and see what makes it tick, take it apart and put it together again, allowing our left and right brains to work together, both learning and exploring at the same time.

## Hypnosis and Hypnotherapy

When we hear the word *hypnosis*, many of us have stereotypical images of entertainers on stage making unsuspecting volunteers behave in strange ways, solely for the amusement of the rest of the audience. At best, it summons up the idea of people going into a deep trance, an altered state of mind with no recollection of what happened during the session. Although trance hypnosis can be effective for self-care and self-improvement, the common reputation it has for leaving people helplessly under the control of the hypnotist can be misleading.

Hypnosis has a valuable role in psychotherapy, and in this context, it is sometimes referred to as *hypnotherapy*.[8] In this form, it is more usual for the subject to remain aware through the session, although mostly in a deep state of relaxation. In this condition, the person is more susceptible to therapeutic suggestions, which can help to release old traumas and habits as well as help install new, positive behaviors. If you are aware of having a traumatic personal history, then please work with a therapist whom you trust. That said, for gentler work, you can still get significant benefit from listening to recorded hypnotherapy sessions.

One form of recording is known as *double induction*. This style uses two interwoven soundtracks, one in each ear, that go deeper into the subconscious by overloading the rational mind. The initial reaction is to try to listen to both at the same time, but the listener can soon relax and go with the flow. This format is especially useful for those of us who are more left-brain analytical in our approach to life.

## What Is a Healing Crisis?

This chapter on self-care would not be complete without talking about the healing process and the fact that sometimes healing can feel just as bad as the original wound. Think of the analogy of spending years carrying a twenty-pound weight on your right shoulder and then suddenly taking it off. In the process of your body adjusting to NOT carrying all that weight, everything is going to feel off as if you are leaning to the left. "Something's not right! What am I doing wrong?" It's just the process of adjusting back to a proper way of being.

There will be occasions when all of the work you do on yourself actually makes you feel considerably worse instead of better. You will find yourself complaining to the universe about how terrible you feel, you don't understand what's going on, you are trying to do everything that you feel you should be doing, you have even just begun this new healing process. That you just started doing something new may be the clue!

It's not that whatever you started doing is not good for you. It may well be one of those occasions when it has stimulated a huge detox for your system, and it is that detox that is causing all of the discomfort, unease, or downright crisis for you right now.

EMOTIONAL AND CHEMICAL IMBALANCES OFTEN FEEL THE SAME WAY ON THEIR WAY OUT AS THEY DID ON THEIR WAY IN.

Sometimes when you feel bad, you may be in the middle of some excellent healing. Remember the way a scab itches as it heals? Emotional wounds can itch in the same way as physical injuries, and often even more intensely. Sometimes when you are in crisis—and especially when you don't understand because you are doing everything you should be doing—it may be that you are doing some rapid healing. Ideally, let yourself go through the experience dispassionately. Welcome it, observe it, allow it to do whatever it needs to do, and let it go. If you have a friend or mentor who understands and can help to guide you through it, great, because it is hard to be objective when you are in the middle of your own healing crisis. If you feel the need to slow things down, use some of the grounding techniques in this book. Physical exercise, showering or Epsom salt baths, time in nature, and heavy foods (meat or carbs) will all help. The discomfort comes from releasing too many toxins, too quickly.

*Healing doesn't mean the damage never existed. It
means the damage no longer controls our life.*
—AKSHAY DUBEY

# Resources

## Mind-body connection

1. *Anatomy of the Spirit: The Seven Stages of Power and Healing* by Caroline Myss
2. *The Creation of Health: The Emotional, Psychological, and Spiritual Responses That Promote Health and Healing* by Caroline Myss and C. Norman Shealy, MD
3. *Heal Your Body* and *You Can Heal Your Life* by Louise L. Hay
4. *Molecules of Emotion: The Science Behind Mind-Body Medicine* by Candace B. Pert

## Zipping

5. *Energy Medicine: Balancing Your Body's Energies for Optimal Health, Joy, and Vitality* by Donna Eden and David Feinstein. An excellent book to supplement all of the exercises in this book.

## Five Tibetan Rites

6. *Ancient Secret of the Fountain of Youth, Book 2: A companion to the book by Peter Kelder* by Peter Kelder. This 2010 edition includes the

original text with additional explanations and commentary making it a better buy than the original version.

## Creativity and Art

7. *Drawing on the Right Side of the Brain* by Betty Edwards

## Hypnotherapy

8. An excellent source of single induction recordings is www.hypno-sisdownloads.com. Among many other titles, this site includes one called "Control Empathy." Although this refers to feeling empathy rather than being an empath, after inducing a state of relaxation, this recording distinguishes between empathy and compassion. It goes on to talk about sending compassionate thoughts out to the people around us. In this respect, it is in harmony with the Light Projector exercise in our chapter "Shielding"; namely, if we stop receiving and start sending energy, we feel better.

# CHAPTER 12

# Meditation, Mindfulness, and Breath Work

By Trevor

> *Meditation: It's Not What You Think.*
> —JON KABAT-ZINN

## Meditation Versus Mindfulness

These days, the terms *meditation* and *mindfulness* are getting intertwined. Meditation has been around for thousands of years and was widely popularized in the West when The Beatles learned Transcendental Meditation in the 1960s. However, over the last few years, the term *mindfulness* has become widespread and is often confused with meditation. Certainly the two terms are interrelated, but there are differences.

The confusion starts with both words having multiple and overlapping definitions. So here's a practical distinction:

- Meditation – A formal mental discipline traditionally undertaken for spiritual development but also practiced in the modern world for health benefits and stress reduction.

- Mindfulness – Any practice of mental awareness. In other words, for example, washing the dishes with mindfulness avoids breaking the china. Mindfulness can also be performed as a formal practice for spiritual growth and health benefits, which is where it overlaps with meditation.

For our purposes here, we will use the word meditation to refer to the formal mental discipline.

## "I Can't Meditate!"

Many of you have already responded in your heads to the title of this chapter with, "But I can't meditate!" You can—really! Your belief that you cannot is a mistake born as a result of misunderstanding what meditation is and how to do it. Stay with us!

## Why Meditate?

Many people learn to meditate for a particular reason, but the potential benefits are many:

- Less emotional baggage; you will find it easier to deal with your stress and that of the other people around you. That includes fewer anxiety issues and reduced depression.
- A more balanced nervous system; it will bring extremes back toward the center. For example, high blood pressure can be lowered, low blood pressure can be raised. Extreme introverts can become more social, extreme extroverts may gradually become more circumspect.
- Better health; most health issues are stress related, so that as the stress falls away, your health will get better. Also, sleep patterns may improve.

- Increased intuition; by definition empaths have unusual abilities, and the likelihood is that you already have or suspect you have abilities beyond just being an empath. The more you meditate, the more those gifts will develop. Applying other exercises from this book will help you sharpen your skills.

Above all else, my advice to anyone is that meditation is the most important thing you can do for yourself and the people around you. By making your world better, you can also improve the quality of life for the people around you.

## Types of Mental Processes

Let's talk about three different kinds of mental processes:

- Contemplating – The process of contemplating is a relaxed awareness that lets the mind drift on various aspects of a topic. The attention floats on the surface of the mind.
- Concentrating – Concentration uses mental effort to either focus on a particular thought or empty the mind to nothingness. This emptying is what is often attempted by beginner meditators and quickly leads to frustration because it works against the nature of the mind. The Eastern term *monkey mind* describes the mind's natural state of being unsettled, restless, and uncontrollable.
- Meditation – The easiest and most effective form of meditation is allowing the mind to transcend activity into a state of restful alertness. This state is sometimes talked about as a fourth state of consciousness, beyond the first three of sleeping, dreaming, and waking. Through effort, concentration works against the nature of the monkey mind. Meditation is about gently and effortlessly bringing the mind back to the point of focus.

## Find a Teacher

Ideally, learn face-to-face from a teacher, and especially one who emphasizes meditation as an effortless technique rather than one of concentration and forcing the mind. Having been practicing transcendental meditation myself for forty years, it naturally has my highest regard.[1] It is also one of the, if not the most, heavily scientifically researched meditation techniques in the world. I can also speak highly of the meditation technique taught by the Art of Living Foundation, which comes from the same Indian tradition.[2] If neither of these options is available to you, there are many good Buddhist meditation teachers who teach for little to no fee. Just ensure that they come from an understanding of meditation without trying or effort. More on that in the tips below.

## Tips for Meditating

If you have to be self-taught, read these tips and try the breath, body, or light meditation techniques outlined below:

1.  **Schedule Time**
    The benefits come from regular daily practice. Certainly meditate once a day minimum, ideally twice a day. If once, morning is best, before the rest of your day invades. If twice, then before eating your evening meal is good, so that the body is not digesting. Pick a specific time so your body can get used to the routine. Twenty minutes is great, but if you need to start off with even as little as five minutes, it is better to get into that routine every day than to meditate irregularly for longer. Meditating late in the day may be relaxing on some days, but it may also be enlivening on others, so you could be left feeling wide awake right before bedtime. Make sure you will be uninterrupted during your meditation so that you need not be concerned about distractions.

2. **Meditate Together**

   Practicing together will keep everyone on schedule better than meditating separately. Also, if you compare meditating on your own to meditating with others, you will quickly discover that your practice will be deeper with more people. If you can find a meditation group in your area where you can regularly meditate with other people, even better. The more, the merrier—literally! Remember, use group meditations to support your daily practice, not replace it.

3. **Sit Comfortably**

   Sitting is better than lying for meditation. The body is used to going to sleep when we lie with our eyes closed. With meditation, the intention is to go into that fourth state of consciousness, restful alertness. You may nevertheless fall asleep occasionally while sitting, especially when you are tired. You will find that your sleep during meditation has a different quality than regular nighttime sleep.

4. **IMPORTANT: Focus, Don't Concentrate**

   The mind will get distracted. All you need to do is gently bring your attention back to the subject of your meditation. It's like using vegetable dye to color a cloth. The dye will not bind at the first attempt, so it is part of the process to bleach the cloth in the sun. It takes many cycles of dying and bleaching for the color to hold fast. So it is with meditating properly: bring the mind into focus, allow the mind to drift, and repeat. Eventually, the qualities of deep meditation will set, like the colors of the cloth. So don't worry about having thoughts. Do not try. Let it be . . . easy!

5. **Don't Try, Don't Expect, Don't Empty the Mind**

   Meditation is a process, not a goal. When the mind wanders, which it does naturally, gently and easily bring it back. Did you have a great experience in a previous meditation that you want to recreate? The one way to guarantee that it won't happen is by trying to repeat it. The most common misconception about "right" meditation is the idea of emptying the mind and experiencing a profound quiet. NO! Expecting to empty the mind is trying to reach the goal without going through the process. Remember to be aware of the mind wandering, and simply bring your attention back to the point of focus each time. This is a skill. Be patient; the inner quiet will come with practice.

6. **Ideally, Stretch and Breathe Then Meditate**
   Stretching loosens the muscles and tendons, allowing you to sit more comfortably. It starts the process of "going inward" and brings added attention to the body. Deep breathing slows the heart rate, relaxes the muscles, focuses the mind, and readies the body for meditation. That said, if it is a matter of time, meditation is THE most important thing you can do for yourself.

## Breath Meditation

The focus of this meditation technique is on the breath. Be aware of your breathing. When the mind wanders, bring the attention gently back to the breath. Don't be concerned about having thoughts. When you become aware of these thoughts, simply bring the attention back to the breath.

Do not count the breath, do not force the breath. Just be conscious of it. If the breath seems to be so shallow as to have all but stopped, just be aware; it will naturally pick back up. It is all about awareness, so when you notice that you have been thinking about something else, just come back to the breath.

If you have physical sensations while you are meditating, relax the attention from the breath and instead use that feeling in the body as your focus for several minutes. Once you have given the body the attention it is craving, the sensation will ease, and you can go back to focusing on your breath.

Be regular in your practice, daily or ideally twice a day. It is better to be consistent for a few minutes every day than to meditate for longer periods on a more infrequent basis.

## Body Meditation

This is an excellent meditation for when you are stuck—stuck in life, a job, a relationship, etc. It can be with an emotional reaction to a situation or with a physical pain. This helps you break the cycle of having one useless thought after another where nothing you can think of works. Getting back into your body can create the shift you want.

In the breath meditation above, we talked about the possibility of having physical sensations while you are meditating and turning the attention from the breath to the body; we begin this meditation here. If you are stuck in your head with strong emotions or a difficult relationship, sit or lie down quietly and ask yourself, "Where does this exist in my body?" It may take you a few minutes to locate the physical sensations, especially at first.

When you use this meditation for physical aches and pains, then it is obviously much easier to locate the sensation. Most of the time we resist pains in the body, they get in the way of living life. Yet these pains are trying to tell us something that we need to listen to, and it's not that we have a deficiency of over-the-counter, pain-killing medication in our system! What we resist persists. Our body is telling us something; this exercise gives us a chance to listen.

This is one of the very few forms of meditation we would recommend practicing lying down. The first step, locating the sensations in the body, is easier when you can just let go. Mentally scan the body to sense where there is any tension. You may have to ask, "Where does this exist in my body?" Wait for the answer. Be patient; it may take several minutes to get a response. Keep scanning your body until you do. If there are multiple areas, pick one—usually the one that seems to be craving the most attention. You can always come back to the other areas later.

When you find an insistent sensation in the body, let your attention rest there. Do not judge it; do not try to fix it. Be with it as a silent witness to however it expresses itself. Simply thank it and set it free. Continue to observe, continue your acceptance, and again, set it free. This may change the intensity; the pain may move to a new place in the body; all that is absolutely fine. The sensation may even disappear in a few minutes. Sometimes you may only notice later in the day that the feeling has gone or that the conflict in your head seems different. Older aches and pains may take many sessions. Set a time for how long you want for each session, and like all meditation sessions, it is better to practice for a short amount of time on a daily basis than a longer period irregularly.

## Light Meditation

This light meditation has the following attributes:[3]

- It is quick. It takes anywhere from twenty seconds to one minute while still being long enough to engage mental focus.
- It is cumulative. Like all meditations, the more you do it, the stronger it becomes.
- It can be used when you get up in the morning or go to bed, eyes open or eyes closed, when you're feeling dull, when you're feeling happy—whenever.

The process uses the following steps:

1. Visualize a circle of light in the shape of a large hula hoop of light over your head. Move this down from above your head to below your feet, and then move it back up over your head. That is one vertical set. Do three of these. You are now inside a cylinder of light.
2. Visualize a second circle of light (or a larger hula hoop of light) to the right of your body (bigger than the first). Move this from the right side of your body to the left, and then shift it back to the right. That is one horizontal side set. Do three of these. You now have a second cylinder of light around you, larger than the first one.
3. Visualize a third circle of light (or a huge hula hoop of light) at the front of your body (larger than the second). Move this circle or

hoop from the front of your body to the back, and then return it to the front. That is one horizontal depth set. Do three of these. You are now surrounded by three cylinders of light.

Add whatever you wish to this light. You may want to put guardians or angels around it or over it. You can put a two-way mirror around yourself if you feel exposed; you can see out, while the people around you cannot see in. Visualize light rays going out from you to other people if you feel isolated. Adapt this exercise for whatever you feel you need.

You may use this light meditation around yourself, your friends, your family, your house, your neighborhood, your car, a meeting you're in, or even around the whole planet. Anything you wish, be as creative with it as you want to.

## Breath Work

Breath work has many benefits. Most importantly are the two that follow:

1. Breath work releases toxins, refreshing the mind and body.
2. Breath work relaxes the mind and body in preparation for meditation.

We still maintain that meditation is the most important regular routine you can do for yourself. Breathing can help you settle into a consistent practice, especially if you find meditation to be challenging initially.

### A Simple Breathing Exercise

We introduced awareness of the breath as a fundamental meditation in the previous chapter. As a breathing exercise, we are going to add a count.

As an easy introduction, start by breathing in deeply for a count of four (approximately four seconds), hold for a count of four, out for a count of four, hold for a count of four, and repeat. This format of 4-4-4-4 is sometimes referred to as *square breathing*. If holding for the count of four is uncomfortable, feel free to shorten the length of the holding of the breath.

You can start off doing this exercise for a few minutes counting your breath, and then, when you are ready, start meditating. Breathe as deeply as is comfortable while counting; do not force the breath. When meditating, drop the count and just sit comfortably with your relaxed awareness on the breath. Let your breathing be natural and effortless while you are meditating.

### Which Count Should I Use?

Different teachers may teach different rhythms. As you become more confident, try moving to a count of in for 4, hold for 4, out for 7, hold for 1 and repeat; 4-4-5-3 is another option. Once you become more experienced, your lung capacity will increase, and you may naturally be inclined to slow down, making each breath last longer.

### Alternate Nostril Breathing

This intermediate technique is often taught in yoga classes. The Indian name for it is *nadi sodhana*.

The steps for practicing alternate nostril breathing are as follows:

1. Place your left hand palm up on your lap.
2. Place your right index finger between your eyebrows
3. Use your right thumb to close off your right nostril.
4. Inhale slowly through your left nostril.
5. Pause for a second.
6. Now close your left nostril with middle and ring fingers and release thumb off your right nostril.
7. Exhale through your right nostril.

8. Now, inhale through your right nostril.
9. Pause.
10. Use thumb to close off right nostril.
11. Breathe out through left nostril.
12. Repeat from step 3 above.

The steps 3-12 form one round. Start slowly with a few rounds and, as you feel comfortable, increase to five or ten minutes. Never force the breath. When you finish, sit quietly for a few moments, then gently start your meditation practice.

## Advanced Practices

There are a great many more advanced forms of breath work. Many have come from centuries-old Eastern traditions.

Although much information can be found in book form or on the Internet, we strongly recommend that you learn directly from a teacher. The more powerful any technique is, be it breath work or meditation, the stronger the emotional and physical release process can be. The results can occasionally be overwhelming in the short term, and it is far better to have a skilled teacher guiding you through the experience.

# Resources

1. Transcendental meditation: www.TM.org
2. Art of Living: www.artofliving.org
3. This light meditation came from Cosmic Awareness Communications: www.cosmicawareness.org.

# CHAPTER 13

# Manifesting—An A.P.P.L.E. a day

By Trevor

> *Our only limitations are those we set up in our own minds.*
> —NAPOLEON HILL

An A.P.P.L.E. a day is a mnemonic for a formula to manifest what you want in your life:

**A** – Appreciate
**P** – Perfect . . .
**P** – . . . Precision
**L** – Let go
**E** – Enjoy the fruit

Let's look at each of these in turn

## A. – Appreciate

Appreciate what you already have—attitude of gratitude. When did you last enjoy giving a gift to someone who wasn't grateful? How did you feel about giving to them the next time? The universe feels the same way about giving to us!

There is scientific evidence that expressing gratitude for just two minutes a day for twenty-one days can make a significant difference to your outlook on life. Where attention goes, energy flows; the more attention you put on being grateful, the more you find that you have to be grateful for. You can express your gratitude in the privacy of a journal or set up an exchange system with a good friend where you share your "gratitudes of the day" with each other. You could even post three things you are grateful for each day on your favorite social media site, to support and encourage support from your friends. Hopefully, you will even inspire some of them to start doing it with you. Then, at the end of twenty-one days, you can ask yourself if maybe you want to continue.

Creating a "gratitude jar" as a variation on this theme is a recent trend. The idea is to put a piece of paper into the jar each day with at least one thing you are thankful for. At the end of the year, or on any day during the year that you need a boost, you can go through the list and look at all your reasons for being happy. You can be grateful for global or personal things, from life-changing events to the little things like seeing a butterfly. Do you want to practice expressing gratitude to someone? Make one day a week a Random Act of Gratitude Day.

The only rules are the ones you choose to create or break. Have fun with the idea.

## P.P. – Perfect Precision

Know what you want! Let the universe know you are fussy and particular. Has anyone ever given you the perfect present without you saying anything about what you wanted? It's wonderful to be given a much desired, unexpected gift, but if we don't drop some very explicit hints along the way, then it is more likely that we will be surprised with something that is less than ideal.

"You want more money? Here's a nickel. I've given you more money . . . Oh, you wanted more than five cents? Then how much do you want?" Be specific, or better still, ask for what you truly want the money for. The only meaningful purpose of receiving money is to exchange it for goods or services that you want. Just wanting more money without being clear about why you want it is a great recipe for being unhappily wealthy.

Be specific about what you want!

## L. – Let go

Not letting go is like sitting in the backseat of the car yelling, "Are we there yet?" before your parents have even driven away from the house. It's like climbing a ladder without wanting to release your handhold on each rung. In the martial arts, they teach that a relaxed muscle is capable of much more than a tense muscle. Similarly, it's much harder to receive with a clenched fist rather than an open palm. Not letting go does not help the flow of energy.

From the concept of letting go, we move on to talking about the principle of non-attachment. When we are attached to something or someone, we give away a piece of our power. The common misunderstanding of non-attachment is giving up possessions. However, it is less about owning nothing, and more about not being owned BY something.

Attachment to possessions is just another way to give up our power to something outside ourselves. Enjoy your possessions; just remember that they are playthings and are in no way connected to who we truly are at a soul level. What is true for the objects in your possession is equally true for the objects of your desires.

Let go!

## E. – Enjoy the fruit

It is in that space of letting go (the same restful alertness that meditators know so well) that the serendipity happens. Having done all of the above, enjoy the fruit!

An APPLE a day...

A – Appreciate what you already have

P – Perfect ...

P – ... Precision about what you want

L – Let it go, allow the flow

E – Enjoy the fruit (having done all of the above)!

# CHAPTER 14

# Crystals

By Abbigayle

*Crystals amplify the consciousness.*
—SHIRLEY MACLAINE

Many people choose to bring crystals into their lives to help them with emotional, spiritual, and metaphysical work.[1] Just as everyone has a signature vibration, crystals have their own individual properties. A crystal's color, clarity, and strength, as well as other qualities, provide its unique vibration for healing and energy work. For this reason, stones can be used for their energetic values in just the same way as light and sound therapy. Depending on how you choose to use them, they can be used to store or channel vibrations, as well as repel or retune lower vibrations.

Crystals can be very helpful as you begin to deepen your understanding of your unique gifts. You may want to use them to help you with basic shielding practices until you are more confident in your ability to process energy in a healthy way.

You will read a lot in this book, and elsewhere, about crystals (for example, quartz, amethyst, and tourmaline) being particularly good for one job or another. You will start to notice a lot of overlaps between stones and their different purposes. The reason for this is because while some crystals are more vibrationally tuned to a particular type of healing work, it is ultimately a connection between the crystal and the healer that is most important. Therefore when choosing your first crystal, start by asking yourself, "Which one feels good?"

Your first choice of crystal should be a grounding stone. The best one for you will make you happy all over just by looking at it. You may feel that it's pretty or you like the color, perhaps it feels good to the touch; go with the one that attracts you, for whatever the reason. Once you have chosen your first stone, spend some time with it; you may even want to carry it in your pocket or wear it as a necklace.

When you begin using crystals for more precise work, it will be helpful to know which stones are useful for that specific purpose, to narrow your search. Then choose a stone from the group used for that purpose. Grounding, shielding, and intuition development are some of the most common uses for empaths and healers who are starting to work with stones.

Crystal quartz is the most universal of all and can work as an amplifier for an intention. If you plan to work with stones, you should consider finding a crystal quartz point (a small, raw specimen that is tapered at one end) that draws you. Learn to work with it before exploring other crystals with a more specialized vibration. Many other healing crystals, such as amethyst, are variations of quartz.

It is important to charge your crystal with the intent for which you want to use it. For example, if you have chosen a piece of quartz and wish to use it to release old habits, you would simply spend time meditating with it and envisioning releasing the behavior. Imagine that when you are tempted to react in the old way, the crystal will vibrationally remind you of your higher goal.

## Grounding Crystals

Grounding crystals help you feel connected to the earth, centered and balanced. You can choose a stone for grounding any time you are feeling loopy, unfocused, or scatterbrained.

- Hematite and smoky quartz both bring a deep grounding energy. Rose quartz can help retune any heavy vibrations within your space.
- Red jasper is especially good at bringing mental and emotional stability and a warm feeling of security.
- Garnet increases your internal energy and triggers an intense inner joy while helping you stay in the present moment and, therefore, is an excellent tool for centering.
- Aquamarine brings a vibration of inner peace and self-love. It can also be useful for emotional shielding and brings in the assistance of the Universe for protection and guidance.
- Carnelian is known as "the stone of grounding." It encourages a warm feeling of euphoria and a relaxed, stress-free state. It reduces fear and anxiety, which is not only useful for grounding after a stressful event, but can also be used proactively to shield against these heavy emotions in the first place.
- Tiger's eye is a great stone to keep on hand during any potential high-stress situation, as it brings an energetic pull toward your natural center.

## Shielding Crystals

This brings us to shielding. Empaths are particularly talented at picking up emotions such as anger, guilt, insecurity, and fear, to name but a few. By introducing crystals that can help block and absorb these and many other "sticky" emotions we may encounter, we can increase our ability to shield ourselves. When we are discussing crystals and their shielding properties, there are two types: There are crystals that block unwanted or dense vibrations, and there are the ones that absorb those same energies. These stones can be used either separately or more often in conjunction with one another to help keep your personal space clear and free of unwanted energies such as others' negative emotions.

- Black tourmaline is useful for redirecting negative vibrations. In other words, it can help strengthen the intention we have already set for those unwanted feelings to bounce off our energetic bubble.
- Labradorite can help to clear your energetic aura by absorbing heavy emotions that may cloud it.
- Selenite helps you develop your shielding abilities by stimulating certain brain activity to encourage inner awareness and help you obtain a higher state of self-awareness and being. That's a fancy way of saying it can help you know the difference between what's "yours" and what's "mine" energetically and turns your own information volume up.
- Prehnite can also help with this by turning the empathy volume down. It allows sensitive people to be sympathetic without being empathic and absorbing the energy.
- Amazonite is a powerful filtering stone as well. It brings a feminine and masculine energy at the same time, allowing us to see a situation from both sides. In the case of empathic energy exchange, it enables us to empathize with someone (a feminine quality) but to remain emotionally detached from the outcome (a more masculine talent).

## Releasing Crystals

Many of the things we are trying to shield and protect ourselves from as empaths can become stuck within our aura when we come in contact with someone else's heavy emotions. Imagine a shaggy dog running through the undergrowth. They pick up briars and burrs in their coats that become tangled and matted. This can happen with feelings as well. So, just as we have to remove the burrs from our pets' coats, it is important to remove any emotions that may have become stuck to us throughout the course of day-to-day living.

- Rhodonite has been called "the rescue stone" by healers. It carries a powerful healing vibration that encourages forgiveness and compassion for oneself and others. It also can help you release fear.

- Morganite is the crystal of Divine Love. It promotes abundance within your heart and encourages prosperity in the form of love. It helps release any unhealthy emotional patterns developed in relationships (with yourself and others). It helps you redevelop your sense of trust and find your inner strength.

- Malachite is very useful in the release of suppressed emotions. As empaths, we are so sensitive to the energy around us that we tend to want to protect others from our own negative emotion. So we shove our emotions down, bottle them up, sweep them under the rug, and let them eat away quietly at us instead. Malachite will help you release those bottled-up emotions, and in doing so, it will also make room for more prosperity.

- Black obsidian is known to absorb any negativity that it contacts. Therefore, it can be used to release any unwanted energy that may be within your space. Apache Tear Drop is a form of black obsidian that is especially useful during a period of loss or mourning. The legend of the Apache Tears speaks of the death of seventy-five Apache warriors and the sorrow of their wives and loved ones. It is said that one who carries this stone will never have to cry again, due to the tears of those Apache women.

- Amber is useful for cleansing the body, mind, and spirit to work on physical symptoms associated with emotional distress. It can help absorb pain and gently realign your nervous system. It can also flush your system of the toxic residue from negative emotions within your body. Your kidneys, liver, gallbladder, and stomach are just a few of the systems that can be affected by emotional blockages.

- Amethyst is a jack of all trades for the most part, but I have chosen to save it for the release work because of its incredible healing properties of the mind. Known as "the sobriety stone" for its soothing vibrations, it helps to break any old habits that no longer serve you. It raises your awareness, giving you the foresight to see the things you need to release. It allows you to purify your energetic space and begin your journey again with a clean slate.

- Thulite is the stone to work with if there are any illnesses or PTSD issues related to childhood abuse or abandonment. It has a soft and gentle vibration that works deep within your system. It nurtures the ability to find a balance between what happened in the past and what you want for your future, lovingly giving you the tools to heal and love your wounded self in the way that you need.

## Intuition Crystals

As empaths, the most powerful tool we have is intuition. When we learn to listen to our inner voice, we naturally begin to attract a higher vibration. This is why the best thing you can do to protect yourself from unwanted emotions is to develop your natural intuitive power; many crystals can offer help with this. However, it is important to note that they can only raise the volume of your inner voice. It is up to you to start by recognizing your natural gifts and emotions.

- Labradorite is said to connect to the Aurora Borealis, the Northern Lights. It functions as a vibrational bridge between your ego and your higher self. When used during meditation, it can help to raise your awareness and allow you to view a situation from the perspective of your higher consciousness.

- Moonstone carries the natural vibrations of the moon. An extremely personal crystal, it is like the blunt friend who doesn't sugarcoat things. It doesn't raise or lower any vibration; it only brings clarity to what is. Moonstone is very talented in bringing into the light parts of you that were once hidden. For empaths who are growing, it can be very useful during self-exploration. It can help someone find their gifts and perhaps blockages that are hindering them from using those gifts for the higher good.

- Lapis lazuli is called "the stone of wisdom" by healers. Its intense vibration resonates deep within the third eye, opening your consciousness to a new light. It is extremely helpful in self-development because it opens you to an inner truth and encourages self-expression and awareness. When working with this stone, it can be useful to explore more creative outlets, such as writing or painting, to discover your inner wisdom.

- Tiger's eye brings a different kind of vibration by working to integrate the emotional-spiritual connection to the logical-physical side of your being. It is the balance between intuition and logic, allowing you to reflect outwardly what your intuition is inwardly saying. It also helps to quiet the negative self-talk that sometimes can override our true inner voice.

Because these crystals are continually absorbing energy, it is important to cleanse them regularly. This can be done in several ways: smudging with smoke, burying them in the ground, using natural spring water, etc. Be sure to use a cleansing method that is appropriate for each crystal because some will fade in sunlight, others will dissolve in water, and these are just two examples of the ways you could damage your stones. You can get more information about ways to cleanse your crystals from your local crystal shop or online.

## Making a Crystal Grid

After you have a few crystals, you can either continue to work with them on an individual basis, or you can build a grid to work with them collectively to enhance and amplify your intentions. So first things first. What exactly is a crystal grid? It is a geometric layout of stones and other natural items connecting individual crystals into a network of energy powered by intent and affirmations. In other words, it is a collection of (mostly) crystals laid out and charged with a particular purpose in mind. This collective energy can be much more powerful than using just one or two crystals for an intended goal. By bringing these stones together, you are connecting the energy between what it is you want and the power of your intention to create it.

There are a couple of things you should consider before you begin. First and foremost is space. When you're talking about a pile of rocks in a studio apartment, size does matter. You want to think about where you want to set up your grid. It should be out of the way but not out of sight. You're going to want to leave it in place for a while, so you will want it somewhere that it will be convenient and undisturbed. However, you are going to want to spend time with it regularly, so it doesn't need to be so out of the way that it becomes "out of sight and out of mind." If you live in a smaller space or need it to be movable, building it on a harder surface such as a cake pan or piece of cardboard and then securing the stones with a small piece of clay will make this easier. You can adjust the number and size of your crystals based on the space you have available.

Another thing to consider is time. You probably don't want to begin a new grid during a busy period in your life. Sure, we're always busy these days, but this is not a project to begin when you are in the middle of planning a family get-together or putting in many hours of overtime at work. You must be willing and able to commit the time, for a grid to assist you. I recommend thirty to forty-five minutes a day; this can be all at once or split up in the morning and evening. For some, this may not be possible at first, but I wouldn't advise any less than fifteen to twenty minutes, three times a week, for as long as your grid is open (or active). This time is to reflect on your intentions and any blocks around them and what you can do to move past those blocks, and for envisioning yourself after you have achieved these goals. Imagine this energy flowing from you, into the crystals, and then out into the Universe to manifest. By spending this time with your grid, you are recharging these goals and affirmations as well as vibrationally writing them in stone, so to speak.

When choosing a pattern for your grid, there are several options. Some may feel drawn to sacred geometry, or you may find inspiration in nature from animals, leaves, insects, or even bodies of water; and still others may create their patterns intuitively. I have even seen a few grids with initials and a dollar sign ... there is no wrong way to build your grid. The only thing that matters is what feels right for you; the pattern is only a visual representation of the energy you have created.

The same, of course, is true when choosing what to add to your grid as well. There are no wrong crystals. These stones and other trinkets are simply vessels in which to hold the power of your intention and energy. So let me repeat that the energy you charge them with is the only power these crystals hold. While there is much talk about which crystals are good for what purpose, this is only because they are more receptive to certain vibrational intentions. So while it is helpful to know that tourmaline is good at protecting against negative energies, it can still be used in a grid for something unrelated like creating financial abundance. Put the other way, if you want to build a grid for a particular purpose but do not have "the right stones," go ahead using the crystals you do have. Trust that your intuition and intention will know which stones to use for what purpose.

Now it's time to open your grid:

- Open the space in a way that feels comfortable for you. Lighting candles or incense, smudging the room to clear it of negative energy that may block your intentions, and inviting your Higher Consciousness or inner voice to guide you through the process can all be helpful in this process.

- Breathe deeply and state your intention aloud, or visualize it in your mind and write or draw it on a piece of paper.
- Keeping your purpose in mind with each stone, set up the outer stones first and work your way toward the center.
- Fold up your paper and place it in the center of your grid. Then put your central crystal or *keystone* on top of that.
- The next step is to activate your grid. Use a crystal point (in this case, size doesn't matter) and draw a line between the stones starting from the outside and connecting them to the center. Remember dot-to-dot as a child? This is the same idea; you are just drawing a line from stone to stone. If you don't have a quartz point, you can use another stone from your grid or even your finger will do. The intention is the key here.
- Now your grid is complete and activated. You may feel like adding other things to or around it in order to realign your intentions later. These may be herbs, candles, or other crystals you feel drawn to throughout the cycle. Lunar energy is very conducive to intention and release work, so we recommend drawing on this energy by building your grid with the new moon and returning to it during the full moon for cleansing and recharging your crystals and grid. Use the recharging time to explore consciously what is in need of release, for you to continue moving toward your goals.
- Remember to spend a few minutes each week with your grid, reflecting on your intention and consciously shifting your internal compass toward that end. Ask yourself what you have done today to move toward your purpose? If the answer is "nothing," this is okay! Just readjust your awareness, and start fresh tomorrow. Ask yourself if you ran into any blocks that hindered your progress toward this. If so, what can you release to remove them?
- BE SPECIFIC!!! It is important when working with crystal energy, especially in manifestation and intention work, to be as detailed and

precise as you can. Instead of saying, "I want abundance," it is better to be very clear on what abundance looks like to you. Would you like to see more income? Joy? Love? Peace in your family?

## Trevor's "Rock Envy" Story

Diamonds, emeralds, rubies, and other precious gems have their value for their rarity but also for their energetic vibration. The more common, semi-precious gems that Abbigayle has discussed above also have their own energy. Even ordinary rocks have a vibration that can be useful to us, as I found out for myself.

I was on a weekend writing retreat a week before my mother died. For one exercise, the facilitator sent us off on a hunt to find meaningful rocks, ones that felt significant to us in some way. I felt directed along the drive-way. I looked down at the stone chippings by the side of the road and saw one that looked like it would make a good pendulum or pendant. Really? Ordinary roadside rocks? You've got to be kidding me.

I picked up the stone along with two others beside it and headed back up to the house. The rest of the group shared their stories about how they found their perfect rocks, including a huge lump of quartz crystal. Come on! I picked up ordinary road-building chippings. I can't have done this ex-ercise right.

I was part jealous, part embarrassed. I chose not to share with the group the process I went through to find my own rock.

By the third day after the retreat, the rock was calling to me to be worn round my neck. Okay then! So what is this rock? I went out to the Internet to find out which rocks are used for road building. Not limestone, not gran-ite. Basalt! Next, what are the qualities of basalt? I found an interesting page on the web, but honestly, although the characteristics sounded useful, I re-ally didn't connect with them—not until I had worn the basalt as a pendant around my neck every day for a week. Not until the day after my mother had rejoined our ancestors when I went back and reread the qualities of basalt. Not until I was in the middle of adjusting to the grieving process did I understand those words from the Internet. I quote, "This strong rock lends its strength and endurance to people as they try to continue in difficult times or deal with traumatic changes."

I wore that rock around my neck every day for over two weeks until the homemade pendant broke. We were gathered at my mother's house with family and friends for a small celebration of her life. The cord broke five minutes before I started my eulogy. The rock landed on the floor. It had done its work.

Rock envy? No! I had picked up my perfect rock!

## Resources

1. *The Book of Stones, Revised Edition: Who They Are and What They Teach* by Robert Simmons and Naisha Ahsian

# CHAPTER 15

# Light and Sound Vibrations

By Abbigayle

*If you want to find the secrets of the universe, think in terms of energy, frequency & vibration.*
—Nikola Tesla

## Sound Shielding

In the earlier section on crystals, we went into great detail about vibrations. In this chapter, we are going to elaborate more on the healing effects of vibrations and the ways in which you can incorporate them into your daily routine.

First, what do we mean when we say *healing vibration*? Also, what sources of vibrations are thought of as healing, and why? And of course, I will be discussing the fastest and easiest ways to develop your relationship with and awareness of the vibrational energy that surrounds you.

Healing vibrations are any energetic patterns that benefit the mind, body, or spirit. Everything on Earth has a unique individual vibration. You, me, the rain, the sun, and even your car contain a signature pattern. By using these different frequencies, you can begin to alter your own internal vibration in countless ways to help you in all walks of life, from health and relationships to grounding and spiritual growth. Think of your energetic body as a choir. When all the singers are in sync and in tune, it can be quite lovely to listen to. However, if even one singer is off just a little, then it can be very noticeable. Using vibrational tools will help you ensure that everyone is "singing in key." Everything in this book is designed to help you to tune into and heal your own inner frequency. Grounding, shielding, and meditating are all ways that you can, with little effort, consciously raise this vibration. The following tools can be used to amplify the other techniques from the earlier chapters. I would recommend that you become comfortable with those exercises first, and then incorporate vibrational tools as you feel drawn to them.

Sound or voice vibration is another powerful tool in healing and raising one's frequency. Historically, bells, singing bowls, drums, and chanting have been incorporated in many practices, ranging from the icaros (medicine music) of the native cultures of both Central and South America, to the use of mantras during meditation in Central and Eastern Asia.

Sound healing works by activating and synchronizing parts of your brain that would otherwise not work together. It awakens the parts of your brain that control speech and memory (even when you don't sing along) while simultaneously activating parts of the brain that control movement and planning. By utilizing the unique effect that sound and music has on our brains, we aid in the relief of a vast range of maladies including sleep disorders, anxiety, and PTSD issues, as well as a host of emotional and spiritual blockages.

Our connection to sound vibration is instinctive. This is why we, as parents, buy little sound machines for our children's cribs that mimic the sounds of the womb, because we know that these sounds will soothe the baby. Repetitive sounds, such as those of a heartbeat, waves on the sand, or recorded thunderstorms are just as lulling to our bodies as they are to a baby's.

So how do we utilize this instinctive connection? The formula is an easy one:

$$\text{intention} + \text{frequency} = \text{healing sound.}$$

First, you need to set a clear intention of what you are hoping to heal.

Next, create the sound frequency using soothing music, drums, bells, or any other sound tools.

This vibration can break through any energetic blockages, allowing sound therapy to be especially helpful for chronic physical issues that just don't seem to go away. Think of how an opera singer can shatter a champagne glass just by raising the pitch of their voice. Sound therapy works in much the same way.

A few minutes of listening to quiet music is another easy way to reconnect with the present moment and find your center. If you are drawn to several genres, then choosing between them is also a good way to evaluate the emotions you are experiencing. This goes for the radio as well as media music websites. Sound redirects your vibration.

One thing you can do as a shielding tool is pick one of your favorite songs and sing it in your head. Make sure you pick one that reflects the mood you want, rather than reflecting the emotions you are picking up. The more intensely personal the song is to you, the better. The song will help to drown out the crowd around you.


**Water Sound**

Water sounds are effective for raising energetic vibrations.

The sound of water, like music, triggers a host of internal reactions within our minds and bodies. Imagine, for a moment, the sound of a babbling brook. Just close your eyes, pause, and listen to the water as it laps over the rocks and winds its way through the woods. How do you feel? I'm guessing that even the act of imagining the sound of water has calmed your system. You may feel a little lighter or perhaps just a gentle "ah." This is due to the instinctual connection between humans and the most basic of life elements. There is a subconscious understanding within us that to have water is to be safe.

Empaths are especially drawn to the water's vibrational cleansing because of its healing properties. When we are unable to cleanse ourselves physically, we can ease our discomfort by allowing the sound of water to wash our energetic bodies instead. If you are angry, sad, or just need a mental boost, powerful water sounds such as heavy waterfalls, rushing rivers, or hard waves beating against a rocky shoreline may help push out any negative or lower vibrations stuck in your body. Including rainfall and thunderstorm sounds in your self-care routine during workouts or meditation is a great way to get an energetic two-for-one. Gentler ocean or river sounds can be very lulling and may be worth trying on long, sleepless nights as well.

## Light

Light is vibration. In fact, the colors we see are different frequencies of light waves. The spectrum of visible light runs from the longest wavelengths or lower frequency (red) to the longer wavelengths and highest frequency (white). Light and color therapy have been around for eons within traditional medicine and have recently made their way into Western medicine for the treatment of things such as muscular sclerosis and chronic pain syndromes.

- The simplest way to incorporate light healing into your daily routine is to step out into the sunshine for a few minutes every day (ten or fifteen minutes is sufficient). Even five short minutes in indirect sunlight has been shown to decrease the levels of stress hormones, and when done regularly three or four times a week, it can be helpful in the treatment of depression, anxiety, and a host of other ailments.

- It can also be helpful to include a healing light source within your home. Himalayan salt lamps have many healing properties and emit a soft and healing pink light that can be the perfect tune-up at the end of a long day.

- Mentally drawing light from outside sources is an innate gift we all share. As empaths, we are especially talented at this. Take a few deep breaths and imagine that you are a "light sponge" absorbing positive light and drawing it into your space. You can imagine absorbing warmth from the sun, the uplifting light of a field of flowers, or the soothing light of the moon. Imagine this healing light flowing to the areas of your life or body that need it most. Are you working on releasing something? This light can help break loose a blockage that you have run into. Perhaps you are feeling under the weather. You can imagine this same warm light flowing into the areas of your body that are in need of healing. Of course, the Light Projector exercise in the chapter "Shielding" is another technique for drawing and channeling healing light.

## Colors

Color therapy has also been around for ages and has many applications. You can use color to enhance many forms of healing, and it is especially good when doing any form of energy work. There are eight basic colors within healing therapy, each with a signature vibration that brings its own unique energy within your system.

1. Red is known as "the Great Energizer." One doesn't have to stretch far to understand why. It brings a certain vitality with it and can help release old baggage and clear blockages within your system. With a strong connection to our energies at the base at the spine, it can bring an inner strength and help you remain grounded in trying

times. Red is also very useful when healing your physical body, with its boldness and drive to push through the tough stuff.

2. Orange, sometimes called "the Wisdom Ray," is a two-for-one, in a sense. It works well to help connect body (red) and spirit (yellow). It welcomes enlightenment mentally and physically, both allowing you to heal your physical space and develop the wisdom to understand what it takes to remain healthy in the future. It has a vibrational connection to the energies in the sacrum. This is no coincidence, as it helps give birth to new and creative ideas.

3. Yellow's mantra is, "I am centered," although this may seem counterintuitive to some, as yellow is a color that stimulates the mind. Its vibrational pattern helps awaken your inner inspiration and invites a mentality born from your higher self, and therefore can be especially helpful for anxiety and mental fatigue. It is nourishing and enriches tissues, helping to heal old scars (physical and mental) and inviting healthy growth.

4. Green is famed as "the Universal Healing" color. The halfway point in the spectrum, it represents exact balance and harmony between that which is physical and that which is spiritual. This is why green can be used for a host of conditions ranging from the physical to the emotional and even the metaphysical. Many healers will say, "When in doubt use more green." It is the color of nature and a vibration of the very earth itself. Neither overwhelming to the system nor overly relaxing, it has the power to be soothing to the body and mind. Its vibrations resonate deep within the heart, gently encouraging spiritual and emotional healing with love and forgiveness.

5. Blue is truly the color of honest communication. "The blue ray is one of the greatest antiseptics in the world" according to Dr. Edwin Rabbit, author of *The Principals of Light and Color*. This is probably due to the cooling effect blue has over our energetic system. It can also be quite sedating; this sedating effect can be overwhelming at times and result in a sudden onset of "the blues." We experience the

effects of blue vibrations most strongly in our throats, the center of our personal expressive power. When our throat energies are well balanced and healthy, we are easily able to speak our own truth and communicate our needs without guilt or fear.

6.   Indigo can be thought of as the "color of the clairs." It is used most often for its powerful purifying properties, within both the blood and the mind. It is honest and loyal like blue but incorporates a little stability with a touch of the more logical red tones. Due to its connection to the third eye and pineal gland, it can be a wonderful addition for anyone seeking to enhance and develop a connection to spirit, and it is especially helpful for honing your skills in intuition or any of the clairs.

7.   Violet is a purely spiritual color. There is very little connection to the physical with this color; however, the effects it can have on the mind and spirit are quite amazing. It is the color of higher wisdom and hope. When incorporated into meditation, it can enhance the experience exponentially. By opening the energies at the top of the head, it can help you reach a higher state of enlightenment and self-understanding. Violet encourages an energetic creativity, allowing your imagination to manifest your dreams.

8.   White, the "Divine Light," is perfectly pure in its healing. It is all encompassing in its power, and wraps your entire energetic body with its protective, almost maternal vibration. It's common among those in the spiritual and healing communities alike to send white, healing light to friends and loved ones in times of need. Almost instinctively, we are moved to focus on this purest of lights and to share it as often as possible.

## Reiki and Other Energetic Hands

Hands-on healing techniques are practiced in almost every culture known to man. Like the doughnut, there is some version available almost anywhere.

As we have already learned in previous chapters, everything carries a signature vibration, and the art of healing hands is another way of directing that energy. There are many forms of reiki being taught and practiced today: rainbow, Tibetan, and angelic reiki, to name a few. While they each have their own symbols and an individual culture of healing, the different styles of reiki are all derived from the original teachings of Mikao Usui. Furthermore, there are still more forms of hands-on healing beyond those practiced in reiki. Acupressure, Pranic Healing, many forms of chakra healing, and the *laying of hands* practiced in many religious cultures are all types of manual or hands-on energetic healing work.

Some people even intuit how to work with energy through their hands without having any formal teacher. A person with the gift of healing hands is able to sense the energetic misalignment and direct the vibrational patterns accordingly. They may do this in many ways, either by channeling energy from outside your body and directing it to the places that need more or by reducing energy flow to places that are being overwhelmed by too much flow.

There is a lot of information about the five principles of reiki, and whether you are a reiki master or this is the first time you've seen the word, foundationally, the message is one that anyone can live by. There are various translations of the original Japanese text, but according to Japanese reiki master Toshitaka Mochizuki in his book *Iyashi No Te* (Healing Hands), the principles are as follows:

1. Just for today, do not anger.
2. Do not worry.
3. Be filled with gratitude.
4. Devote yourself to your work.
5. Be kind to people.

We have learned through the course of history, however, that our subconscious minds do not recognize negative adverbs such as "not." For this reason, I have found it useful in my daily practice to convert these ideals into something that my subconscious can recognize and live up to, using the principles of affirmations from our chapter, "Releasing":

1. I am releasing anger.
2. I am releasing worry and fear.
3. I am filled with gratitude.
4. I am fully devoted to my soul purpose.
5. I am kind and compassionate.

By incorporating these humble ideas and embracing them fully, I quickly began to see a difference in not only the way I approached the world, but also in the way others looked at me. Does this mean I never lose my temper? Not even close! It also doesn't mean that I walk around farting sunshine and rainbows when the world is coming apart around me. I get worried. I get angry (more often than I like). I also get lazy sometimes and don't feel like being devoted to anything but a Harry Potter marathon and a bottle of wine, but that's okay, too. It doesn't say I will NEVER; it says, "Just for today," and if today I don't quite make it, tomorrow I will try again. Not one of those statements says, Today I will be perfect!

# CHAPTER 16

# Plants: Herbs, Spices, Oils, and Essences

By Abbigayle

> *Everything on the earth has a purpose, every disease*
> *an herb to cure it, and every person a mission.*
> —Mourning Dove Salish

The history of man and herbal medicine is an ancient one. According to records, herbal medicine is the earliest scientific tradition in medical practice. Many of the most common medications today are historically derived from plants. In 400 BC, Hippocrates made reference to using salicylic tea for fever reduction. This tea was made from willow bark and other plants high in salicylate. Today, this same compound is most commonly referred to as aspirin.

Many of the herbs we discuss in this chapter are available in various different forms: tinctures, teas, capsules, flower essences, or essential oils. Some are even available as candy. The delivery method does not matter greatly; we have simply listed the most common form.

A word of cautionPlease be aware that not all herbal supplements are created equal. Please use caution when purchasing and using over-the-counter herbal supplements, as the contents and doses are not regulated or standardized. There may be more variations in dosages found in the commercial brands than if you were to use whole or loose leaf herbs or essences bought through a private herbalist.[1]

Some herbs and flowers growing in the wild look similar to plants that can be extremely toxic, so please do not attempt to harvest your herbs from the wild without the direction of someone who is trained to know the difference. In this chapter, we will be talking about some very specific uses for a variety of healing herbs. These are simply the author's choice in each category. There are hundreds of herbs that can provide similar benefits. We also recognize that the herbs we've chosen have many more healing qualities beyond the ones we have stated here for the specific purpose of helping empaths. If you are taking medications, please talk to your doctor before taking any herbs or supplements.

## Grounding Herbs

Since we already know that grounding is simply coming back to oneself and finding center, the herbs that can help with this are endless. The goal is to feel cool, calm, and collected. There are several herbs out there that offer soothing relief of anxiety and stress. For grounding purposes, it is important that they don't make you feel sleepy or sluggish.

- Peppermint – Peppermint tea is regarded as the world's oldest medicine that is still used for its many healing properties today. Its soothing aroma begins to ground you even before your first sip. It gently soothes aching and rigid muscles after a stressful day. Peppermint is unique in that it not only fights fatigue and headaches associated with daily stress but is also very useful for warding off insomnia. It has also been shown to help those suffering from migraines. By regularly having some peppermint after each meal, you can see a gradual reduction in stress and fatigue as well as begin to build healthy and more restful sleep patterns. Peppermint also works when sucked as candy, but find one of the pure and natural suppliers that are available.

- Lemon Balm is usually combined with other herbs for calming and grounding effects, though even on its own it's quite diverse in its grounding properties: soothing anxiety, sadness, and muscle tension while bringing fresh eyes to your stressful situation by clearing the emotional fog and renewing your alertness without the anxiety bogging you down. Passion flower is also very useful for this and can be combined with lemon balm. It can ease symptoms of stress such as anxiety, irritability, and mild depression symptoms associated with the daily grind.

- Ashwagandha builds in your system when taken regularly, in a way that can help you manage the emotional overload of everyday stress; in fact, studies have shown a marked reduction in cortisol levels in patients who used ashwagandha regularly.

- St John's Wort has a similar reputation to ashwagandha, BUT although it works very well for some people, it can also have a dangerous downside for others. Particularly for anybody with a tendency towards bipolar disorder, it is far better to avoid this one completely in favor of safer alternatives like ashwagandha.

- No More Drama, Mama Tea
  This is a blend I developed that offers quick relief for the overwhelm and anxiety we experience throughout a stressful day (or in my case, couple of years!):
  - 2 parts ashwagandha
  - 1 1/2 parts peppermint
  - 1 part lemon balm
  - 1 part skullcap
  - 1 part linden flowers

## Meditative Herbs

One way to use these herbs is in smoke form, through smudging or incense, for raising our vibration and supporting a meditative state. Smudging is an oldie, but a goodie. At its core is the burning of herbs to transmute heavy energies. The herbs sage, lavender, sandalwood, or patchouli are just a few smudging possibilities. The dense energies can be any negative emotions possibly stuck on physical objects such as crystals, books, and even clothes. For purposes of clearing negative emotions from your space such as your home or bedroom and from the objects I mentioned, you can start the process in whatever way feels comfortable. Some people call in angels or personal guides to help them clear the space. Next, set light to the herbs— carefully! Imagine that the heavy energy is being drawn into the bundle and transmuted into The Light through the smoke. Watch as the smoke rises from the bundle; you will know that you have successfully cleared your intended space when the stream of smoke goes from a thin, bold line to a wider, wispier kind of flow. This is caused by the balancing of the energy.

Herbs can be used in the form of incense as well; sandalwood is a traditional favorite. Lavender, when burned, also brings a specific vibration that may help you ease into a meditative state and offers mental clarity for retaining information.

There are also several herbs in the form of tinctures, teas, and capsules that support a healthy meditative state:

- Motherwort – This tastes like rotten gym socks when used as a tea, but it is highly effective for meditation and release work. It is very good for severe social anxiety and can safely be taken every ten minutes for a panic attack. It can also be burned for meditative purposes.
- Gotu kola – A sacred herb among yogis, this is said to be the most spiritual of all herbs. With leaves that resemble the human brain, it seems only natural that this plant would offer balance to the left and right sides of your brain. It helps us to build a bridge between

the logical and creative, the masculine and feminine, and the physical and spiritual sides of our bodies.

- Hibiscus – Raises your internal vibrations and invites a feeling of joy to your meditation. It can help you to see better the bright side of your situation or in some cases, help you find the best way out of a situation that has no bright side.
- Marshmallow – Helps you let go of the effort to control life. It aids you in surrendering to the moment and realigns you with Cosmic Order. These can be the most challenging aspects of meditation for some. Helping to relax your diaphragm, it supports the cleansing breath and allows you to let go of the nagging heaviness in the pit of your stomach.
- Come on Inner Peace; I Haven't Got All Day Tea:
  - 2 parts hibiscus
  - 1 part marshmallow
  - 1 part gotu-kola
  - 1/2 part motherwort.

When the tea is prepared, add 1/2 tsp. of ginger, 1 cardamom pod, 1 whole clove, and 1/2 tsp. of ground cinnamon. Steep for five minutes and slowly breathe in the scent as it's brewing. Strain and enjoy.

## Herbs for Physical Support

Some empaths are just as likely to experience the physical symptoms of those around them as they are to experience the emotional ones. Ideally, it is best to recognize immediately when we are taking on physical or emotional input from others. However, sometimes we end up having to treat the symptoms as if they are indeed ours, and in these cases, it is useful to have these herbal remedies for support.

There are a few physical symptoms that seem to occur frequently within the empath community: chronic pain issues such as sciatica or fibromyalgia; migraine disorders; digestive problems such as irritable bowel syndrome (IBS) or gallbladder disease; and any number of symptoms associated with chronic stress. While it would be impossible to make a recommendation for someone with a chronic illness through a book, we feel that there are a few herbs that are worth bringing to your attention:

- Comfrey – This is helpful both as a tea and a compress to relieve mild to moderate muscle pain, bruising, and inflammation. This makes it very useful for people with muscle spasms, sprains, or tension.

- Ginger – One of the most ubiquitous plants on the planet, it can reduce inflammation and swelling, act as a natural antimicrobial to lessen the risk of wound infection, speed healing time, and ease nausea associated with motion sickness, stomach bugs, and morning sickness. It can also be used externally for acne and as a mouthwash for chronic bad breath. It may also help to lower blood pressure by reducing the inflammation associated with hardening of the arteries.

- Oatstraw – A highly replenishing herb that nourishes your nervous system, this is a must-have for anyone who is having difficulty concentrating. It is often coupled with rose hips to support healthy brain function in individuals with ADHD. Their joint power enhances calmness and concentration while helping to quiet the overstimulation of outside forces.

- Burdock root – This is a wonderful cleanser for the liver and a good diuretic to help with waste elimination. Consider using dandelion and marigold as an alternative combination.
  CAUTION: Burdock root can cause severe reactions in individuals who are allergic to daisies, chamomile, or anything in the ragweed family, as they are all closely related. It should be also avoided when pregnant. It can raise insulin levels and MUST NOT be used without medical supervision in conjunction with insulin therapy or for anyone with type 1 diabetes.

- Dandelion and marigold – These are especially useful for detoxing your system after an illness and can be used more regularly to keep your system free of toxic build up. Both are powerful diuretics, so it is important to drink lots of water while using these herbs. When used daily for a week, they will gently cleanse your liver and kidneys as well as rid your body of toxins and any fungal or bacterial growth within your digestive tract.
  CAUTION: Dandelion flowers and pollen can trigger allergies for some people (although tea form may be more tolerable for some). Marigold should not be used by pregnant women, as it may cause contractions.
- Kava Kava – This is very helpful for relieving stress and tension. Beyond that, it has anesthetic properties, so it can be used topically for relief of mild burns. It is also a mild pain reliever, bringing internal relief to minor aches and pains. It can be used as a replacement for benzodiazepines (such as Xanax) and is also useful for reducing the withdrawal symptoms for patients coming off benzos. Furthermore, it is making its way into the supplement aisle after studies have shown that it may help with healthy weight loss. This may have something to do with suppressing the need for emotional eating.

## Herbs for Healthy Rest

Sleep is the most basic of human functions. So why is it so hard for some of us to get the hang of it? We've all been there at least once in the middle of the night, staring at the ceiling, willing our brains to please just SHUT UP! For those of us who are more sensitive to the fluctuating energies around us, we may find that sleep is a fair-weather friend, embracing us in its peaceful state one week and deserting us without a word's notice the next. "Oh, sleep! Why didn't I love you when I had the chance?" These herbs may help you rebuild your relationship with that elusive state of mind.

- Valerian Root – Both gentle in its approach and powerful in its work, valerian is known throughout the world for its soothing and calming qualities. For this reason, it is used for migraines, tension headaches, insomnia, and even some mood disorders. When used with hops, the sedative effects are increased in both, as they have similar properties. Skullcap is lesser known but also boosts the effects of valerian.
- Passion Flower – Making the list a second time, when used in combination with any of the other herbs mentioned in this section, passion flower will help stop the racing thoughts that so often keep us awake.
- Chamomile – One of the best-known herbs as a sleep aide, chamomile works on a dual level, both calming the nervous system and relaxing your muscles, making sleep all the easier to reach. It also has many soothing benefits for the gastrointestinal system.
  CAUTION: Chamomile can cause severe reactions in some individuals, especially those who are allergic to daisies or anything in the ragweed family.
- Turmeric – This spice is rich in antioxidants that naturally help to balance your internal sleep clock. It also has properties that have been shown to reduce insomnia associated with depression and the winter blues. Additionally, it is effective in reducing inflammation caused by stress and unhealthy sleep cycles.
- Poppy – A mild pain reliever and muscle relaxant, it relieves nervousness and hyperactivity. It is safe for all ages and therefore can also be helpful for babies with colic symptoms. Remember to stop using this herb about a week before taking any drug test to avoid a false positive result.
- Catnip – This has been used for over two millennia for its healing properties similar to those of valerian, with the additional benefits of healthier digestion and fever reduction.

- Bedtime for Bonzo Tea

This recipe is for a blend you can make up using:

- 2 parts passion flower
- 2 parts valerian
- 1 part hops
- 1 part catnip
- 1 1/2 parts chamomile

## Tea Time Quick Reference

The following table provides a summary of recommendations for common symptoms. The teas listed can be used individually or as a combination of tea #1 and #2. Again, this is not a definitive list; it is only meant to be used as a guide. We encourage you to discuss your personal needs with your local practitioner to find which teas are best for you.

| Topic | Tea #1 | Tea #2 |
|---|---|---|
| wake up | green | peppermint |
| sleep | kava kava | valerian |
| cold symptoms | mullein | elderberry |
| digestion | ginger | licorice root |
| detox | burdock root | marshmallow |
| nausea | fennel | ginger |
| energy | mint | chai |
| de-stress | lavender | ashwagandha |
| constipation | blackberry root | clove |
| antioxidant boost | rooibos | black |

You will find it more convenient to make up any tea blends in advance. Keep your teas stored in a cool, dry place in an air-tight container. Most, although not all, teas will last for six to twelve months when stored properly. Lavender is a good example of an herb that has a shorter shelf life of only three months.

## Honey

More than just a healthy alternative to sugar for your tea, honey in one of the most ancient medicines known to man. One of the only foods with an eternal shelf life, archeologists have found pots in tombs dating back thousands of years that contained honey that was still as good as new. This "liquid gold" has many healing properties:

- It is a great cough suppressant for adults and older children (NEVER give honey to infants or toddlers). It can be just as effective as over-the-counter cough medicines. By coating the back of the throat, it helps ease the coughing and reduce throat pain.
- It can provide a gentle boost in energy that doesn't give you the "crash" you get with caffeine or sugary drinks.
- Conversely, it can also be a very useful sleep aid. Honey raises your serotonin levels, which provides a peaceful feeling of happiness. When the lights are off, your body converts the serotonin to the sleep hormone melatonin.
- It has been shown to help alleviate allergies. To maximize this benefit, we recommend that you only buy LOCAL, raw honey, as it will be more likely to contain the specific qualities you need in your residential area.
- It is great for skin and wound care. Honey contains natural antimicrobials and can help prevent infection and reduce healing time. For these reasons, it is still used in modern medicine for disinfecting severe burns; it is better than any pharmaceutical alternatives.

When buying honey, there are a couple of things to keep in mind. First, not all honey is created equal. There are many brands out there to choose from, but you want RAW honey. Stay away from pasteurized or processed honey because most of the health benefits are lost during the cooking process. Avoid overheating the honey when using it, so allow your tea to cool to drinking temperature before adding the honey. Beyond this, the flavor can vary widely depending on location, beekeeping practices, and of course, the pollen in the area it was produced.

CAUTION: NEVER give honey to infants and toddlers. It contains Clostridium botulinum bacteria, which is harmless to adults and older children but may lead to infantile botulism in young babies.

## Flower Essences

Flower essences are another natural method of healing that can be a great addition to your tool chest. They gently restore the connection between mind and body by providing the emotional balance that softens and removes unwanted emotions such as fear, worry, hatred, and indecision. Flower essences allow peace and happiness to return to the sufferer so the body is free to heal itself.

The best place for beginners to start is with the most widely-known flower essences, the Bach Flower Remedies.[2] Dr. Edward Bach discovered these in England during the 1920s and 1930s. They are a set of thirty-eight flower remedies as well as the Rescue Remedy products that are great for urgent care situations. They are usually available in your local health food store.

For more advanced work, Trevor's favorites are the Green Hope Farm essences.[3] They seem especially ideal for the more evolved souls, and compared to the Bach Flowers, they reflect how much the consciousness of the planet has risen within just the last one hundred years. Molly Sheehan, the founder of Green Hope Farm, has developed an inventory of nearly a thousand essences, so it does take more work than the Bach Flowers to get to the right choice. However, they are well worth the extra effort and can be a significant asset in keeping emotional balance while fast-tracking your spiritual progress. Green Hope Farm offers individual essences as well as blends that include, for example, ones specifically for healers and empaths as well as more general ones such for anxiety, depression, digestion, and sleep, to name but a few.

The reader should be aware that many other organizations offer great flower essences that you can find with an Internet search or by browsing your local health food store.

## Essential Oils

Have you ever noticed how the smell of fresh baked cookies instantly takes you back to childhood? One sniff and an ocean of memories comes flooding in. The way your grandma let you lick the spoon, you can even almost TASTE the batter and feel the butterflies of anticipation while waiting for the timer to go off to say they were done.

The reason for this time travel is not a complicated one. Scent goes through your brain's cells and triggers the same senses you experienced in that original moment. These scent molecules that connect with your memories can move throughout the body in numerous ways. They carry energetic information to every cell in your body. When used correctly, aromatherapy can help sweep away any emotional residue and toxins along the way. There are many articles on the web about the science behind essential oils and their many uses, but for the time being, let's stick to emotional release.

Whereas the herbal tinctures, teas, and capsules are for internal use, the essential oils must be used EXTERNALLY. You can put them directly on your body, into baths, or use them in aromatic misters.

- Cedarwood oil is very useful in clearing painful emotions associated with memory. It works deep within our cells, where we record emotion, and helps us let go of any past traumas or addictions we may have been holding. For this reason, it is particularly useful in addiction recovery.

- Cypress oil works within your nervous system to calm and soothe you. It can be extremely helpful in releasing anger and hostility and brings a quiet strength in the times of emotional turmoil.

- Lavender can be used in several ways. Inhaling the scent of a few drops of lavender oil has been shown to ease the symptoms of anxiety and panic attacks. It may also help alleviate the flashback-type symptoms of PTSD. Lavender can also be found in supplement form and taken daily for the chronic anxiety that is so common among untrained empaths. Caution: if you suffer from migraines, use cedarwood oil instead of lavender.

- Myrrh oil is a powerful emotional cleanser with a strong connection to the energetic body. It helps release any unnecessary energy that is leaving you off balance or uncentered.

- Ylang-ylang raises your inner vibration to release any sadness or dense energy. It also helps balance your hormones, which may ease the physical symptoms and emotional mood swings empaths may develop with constantly processing other people's energies. This one is also an aphrodisiac, so be warned!

- Tea tree oil (also known as melaleuca) is not traditionally used in an emotional context, but it has so many wonderful healing benefits that we would be remiss to leave it out of this list. It has many anti-inflammatory properties that are very helpful for the skin irritation that is common among highly sensitive people; rashes from eczema, psoriasis, and even poison oak/ivy. It can be diluted and used as drops for ear infections, and when mixed with lavender oil and baby shampoo, it makes for one of the gentlest head lice treatments out there. It has so many beneficial qualities that there are books dedicated to just this one oil.

# Resources

## Plants: Herbs, Spices, Oils, and Essences

1.  Our favorite online store for herbs and other natural essentials is https://www.etsy.com/shop/RavenSongNaturals

## Flower Essences

2.  Bach Flowers: http://www.bachflower.com
3.  Green Hope Farm: https://www.greenhopeessences.com

# CHAPTER 17

# The People Around Us

By Trevor

> *You are the average of the five people*
> *you spend the most time with.*
> —JIM ROHN

Who are the people around you now? If they are a reflection of you, how does that make you feel about yourself? Who are the people who are most suited to your vibrational energy? You will attract different people around you as you raise your awareness. You may possibly learn a lot from looking at the people around you and recognizing the patterns in the people you attract. If you find yourself interacting with the same personality in a different body, the common denominator is you! What is the lesson you need to learn in order to bring different people into your life?

## Empaths as Distorted Mirrors

Do any of the following sound familiar about one or more people in your life?

- You look for reasons to avoid them without understanding why.
- You find yourself unable to think or talk coherently in front of them.

- You feel drained spending time with them.
- You feel guilty because you dislike being with them.
- You feel out of control around them.
- You get a physical reaction around them such as a headache or knot in your stomach.
- You spend too much time thinking about them, possibly to the point of not sleeping properly.
- You find yourself passing their toxicity to your closest friends and family.

Because you are an empath, you are highly sensitive to any mismatch between how they feel and their behavior:

| They feel . . . | They act . . . |
|---|---|
| unloved | overly nice (to get love and adoration) |
| angry or hating | like everything is okay |
| insecure and in emotional pain | rough and tough |
| unaccepted for who they are, inauthentic | wishy-washy and/or they try too hard |
| unworthy | full of insincere praise for you |
| insignificant | by making up interesting stories |
| like a failure | playing the cynic |

Whatever emotion the other person may be avoiding, you will likely be feeling it yourself in some form or another. The more they are suppressing their feelings, the more intensely you are likely to feel them. When we mistakenly think that the energy is our own, our intellectual understanding of what is going through our body will be based on our own life experiences; this is our mind's way of labeling why we feel a particular way.

For example, someone around you may be feeling anxious about money, and you start feeling like you have to hide out and play small. That person may be feeling angry, and you start raging over automated customer support from a company you are dealing with.

Emotionally, we take on the feelings of the people around us, but mentally, we put our own justification on those feelings.

## The Empath and the Toxic Person

The confused empath often has unhealthy people around them and at worst, bonds with the type of personality that is just plain toxic to them. Any person who is overly self-involved, often vain and selfish, lacking in empathy, and unconscious of deficits in their own personality is toxic. They may even come across as being physically or emotionally abusive.

The ongoing theme as to how they make you feel is how they feel about themselves. One of the most common reasons for their toxic behavior is because they are coming from a lack of emotional maturity, not trusting the world, and using attack as their prime form of defense.

The following types of toxic people, using the acronym BAITERs, is adapted from Dr. Phil McGraw.[1] We have added to the six types the way in which each of the BAITERs can make empaths feel in the process of interacting with them:

- **B**ackstabbers – You feel defensive, untrusting, as if the world is out to get you.
- **A**busers – You feel small and very inadequate. You start comparing yourself to others. You find yourself wanting to make excuses for them and blaming yourself for their behavior.
- **I**mposters – You wonder about where you stand as if you are always on shaky ground. You start questioning yourself about who you really are.
- **T**akers – You feel completely insufficient to look after their needs.

- **E**xploiters – You feel like you owe everything to them, and you can't do enough to make it up to them.
- **R**eckless – You feel protective toward them because they can't take care of themselves unless you jump in for them.

## The Empath and Toxic Relationships

Just because the other person doesn't fall into one of the categories above, the relationship itself may still have fallen into a toxic pattern. How do you know you are in a toxic relationship, romantic or otherwise, with another person?

- You are given, and take, more than your fair share of responsibility for everything in the relationship, especially everything that goes wrong.
- You consistently feel invalidated. They're right; you're wrong.
- You consistently feel guilty for not doing enough, for not being enough, around this person.
- You feel drained being around them, yet you keep on pumping more energy into the relationship.
- The other person has a dysfunctional streak that they don't acknowledge, yet it's obvious to everybody else around them!
- You give, they take. Period.

Why do you get sucked in, time and time again?

- You are an empath, so consciously or unconsciously you are a healer. By definition, the toxic person is wounded, and so you naturally take it upon yourself to help them because you feel their pain.
- If you don't realize that the self-doubts are not yours, you are constantly beating yourself up, convincing yourself that you are not worthy of anything better. You are an empath, so you take on their emotions.
- The only way to mix oil and vinegar is to keep stirring them. In the same way, the empath feels in a constant state of chaos as they try to

stay with a toxic person. This can be true to the point that the reason the empath stays is because they fear the emotional storm of leaving.

It may be time to admit that you are only human and that you cannot help the person from inside the relationship with them. Sometimes you just have to love them from a safe distance.

How do you get out?

- Awareness is always half the battle. Once you recognize the pattern, you can change it.
- Don't argue for things to be different. People, ourselves included, can never talk our way out of a situation that our actions took us into. You will never convince a narcissist to change by talking to them. They will say anything to stop you from changing. Do not believe them until you see them behaving differently for a significant time period.
- Trust your instincts, and remember that it is your nature to absorb the other person's feelings. You can never change that which is not yours, and you are absolutely not responsible for changing another person.
- Know that you deserve better. It is time to make different choices.

We should mention that many empaths developed their skills at a very young age as a survival technique when dealing with toxic parents. Those same parents may have had psychic talents themselves but never learned what those abilities were or how to use them. In their confusion and frustration of dealing with the energies they were picking up from their environment, they most likely passed their empathic talents, along with everything else, on to the next generation through both nature (DNA) and nurture (behavior). It is a blessed empath who has been able to grow up as the offspring of a stable or thriving empath and has therefore been able to develop their own talents in a healthy environment. Since empaths are often attracted to toxic people, it is possible you had both an empath and toxic parent.

## The Energy Sponge

Some people are not so much toxic as much as they simply drain energy. They thrive on soaking up energy from their environment, and most empaths will unwittingly provide everything they can. Some energy sponges may indeed be toxic and should be avoided as quickly and completely as possible. Others may be good people who are a beneficial part of your world and who you will want to keep around you. In order to be around them, you will need to intensely practice many of the self-care techniques that have been shared in this book.

You may recognize some of the following types. Some of them are the milder versions of the toxic types given above:

- The debater—"Let's argue." By engaging in an argument with this energy drainer, they win just by riling you up . . . and they'll never admit you are right anyway. Can you let them win before you even fight?
- The abdicator—"You deal with it." They spend most of their days in another realm, avoiding the responsibilities they committed to when signing up for a human body. They will happily let you take on their responsibilities for them. Don't! Can you live your own life and not be responsible for theirs?
- The invalidator—"Mine's bigger and better than yours." These people insert their thoughts, relevant or not, into any conversation and turn the spotlight on themselves. Regardless of their chronological age, they will remind you of a young child desperately looking for attention and validation. You can try saying, "I have such admiration for anyone who can sit quietly and listen to a conversation for a few minutes before they jump in." To slow them down maybe try saying, "I feel [frustrated, confused, etc.] when you interrupt a conversation." Can you find a way to draw the appropriate boundaries that benefit both you and them?

- The victim—"Help me." Whereas the abdicator is uninterested in the mundane world, this person appears to care deeply but feels unworthy and incapable of doing anything for themselves. They look to you to do everything for them and, if you are willing, there will be no limit. Can you support them without co-dependently enabling them?

- The martyr—"You owe me." This type lives their life serving other people, and they try to enslave you into expressing gratitude to them. It does not matter that you never asked them to be a martyr in the first place. They signed you up for the job of serving them by everything they think they did for you. Mothers are notoriously good at this role—not all, but certainly some. If are you feeling guilty and don't understand why, it's a sign you are dealing with a martyr. Can you take care of any responsibilities you feel you have to this person without sacrificing yourself? Can you avoid the trap of becoming a martyr or victim yourself when dealing with this type of person?

- The excuse maker—"Yes but." They are in a constant push-pull of trying to conform to what they think others want from them while trying to prove themselves right. They want your input solely so they can reject it. Can you be more inquisitive about what they think rather than sharing what you think?

- The Cleopatra (Queen of Denial)—"I'm fine." This type claims to have no issues even though there is an underlying theme of dissatisfaction. They are out of touch with their shadow side, yet the darkness within us is part of being human. You will likely feel drained from unconsciously sensing the reality that they are denying. Additionally, they do not feel particularly alive in their life, so neither will you in yours when you are in relationship with them. Can you share more of your own issues and guide them to be more in tune with theirs?

If your answer to the questions at the end of each type is, "No. I've tried that, and it isn't working," then maybe it is time reevaluate the relationship; try something different or simply walk away. Your true friends will be the people with whom each of you can be honest about your needs. If you can all be circumspect about your behaviors, value each other for being real, and hold one another accountable, you will grow together and create something wonderful.

CAUTION: The labels shared here are to help you recognize the energy and, through that recognition, empower your response to the other person. They are not to be used as judgments to put on others to make them wrong—tempting though that may be!

These people show up in our lives to reflect our own shadow side. Observe how your thoughts and emotions are reflected in the world around you. This will enable you to change yourself. By understanding these labels, you will be better able to find an appropriate response to a situation rather than having a knee-jerk reaction. Every relationship in your life is there for a reason—especially the difficult ones. Can you find the lessons buried in the challenges?

## A Healthy Vibe Tribe[3]

As you move from being a confused empath, through being a stable, to thriving, the people around you will change. A confused empath will likely gather similar souls around them in an attempt to feel seen, heard, and validated. As you start to thrive, you are far more likely to surround yourself with others skilled in their abilities. Some people will naturally move away from you because they no longer feel comfortable in your vibration, or you will move away from them as you find that you can no longer tolerate theirs. Change is rarely easy; however, as new people come into your life, be prepared to let some of the old ones go. Sometimes you may have to empty your glass before you can receive a refill. The Universe will help you change. You have to be a willing participant in the process.

It is useful to recognize three groups of people around you:

- Your teachers and mentors – These are the people you can learn from, who have more wisdom and experience in a particular area than you. It is good to remember two things: first, they are still human, and second, they will probably still be learning from you. The higher the pedestal that you put them on, the further they have to fall, and sooner or later you will have to balance everything you have learned from them with the recognition that they are still human and capable of having human flaws.

- Your peers – The soul friends with whom you can dialogue, sharing your problems with them as they share theirs with you. It is a relationship of both giving and taking. We each have our ups and downs, so there will be times when the friendship will feel unbalanced. If you feel like you are being drained, take some time out for yourself to disconnect from the relationship, recharge, and reconnect to Source. Though be wary if it feels like the relationship has shifted to one side for too long.

- Your students – These are the people who can learn from your wisdom and experience. As an empath, your nature is to want to give. You probably need no encouragement to do so; just ensure that the experience is nourishing rather than draining. It is good to remember three things: first, try not to care more about teaching them than they care about learning from you. Second, you were once where they are now, and third, you may still have things to learn from them. They may try to put you on a pedestal; do your best to avoid thinking that you deserve it. The higher the pedestal, the further you will have to fall, and being human, sooner or later you will have to realize that you are still flesh and blood and capable of having your own flaws. If you do end up lying on the ground at the foot of your pedestal, you will have a crowd around you gawking and laughing at your expense. This, too, is usually good for growth!

## Resources

1. *Life Code: The New Rules for Winning in the Real World* by Dr. Phil McGraw

2. *How to Defend Against Emotional Muggers* by Martha Beck http://marthabeck.com/2014/02/defend-against-emotional-muggers

3. Elise Lebeau's Empath Community http://empathcommunity. eliselebeau.com.

   This site includes a very active set of discussion groups that can provide excellent support and a sense of community for a new empath.

# CHAPTER 18

# Parenting an Empath Child

By Abbigayle

> *You are the bows from which your children*
> *as living arrows are sent forth.*
> —KAHLIL GIBRAN

## Recognizing an Empath Child

Okay, so I'm an empath . . . is my child one, too?[1] The most likely answer to that question is, YES! These gifts are usually, though not exclusively, passed down through the mother's bloodline and can, in some cases, skip a generation. So if you think that your child may be an empath, even if you are certain you are not, I would suggest you look deeper into the family history of both sides of the bloodline. You may not think of the older generation as being empaths; however, they may well display some of the mental health challenges that are all too often symptomatic of confused empaths.

So how do you know if your child is an empath? Let's start by going over some of the most common signs in younger children:

- Extreme sensitivity to the emotions around them. This may seem obvious, but for children, this can be very painful, especially if there is a lot of anger or anxiety within the home. Sometimes these children will complain of aches and pains that are unexplained, usually in their backs, necks, or arms. Growing pains may last a day or two; however, these will either last much longer or will reoccur over time in the same places.

- Confusion or insecurity about the world around them. This may translate into overly shy behavior or clinginess. This child is often afraid to meet new people and doesn't handle crowds well, including stores and supermarkets, which often leads to tantrums in public.

- Crying for no reason. So Tommy's playing with toys on the floor while you're watching the news. Suddenly he's crying uncontrollably and can't tell you why. It's very possible that without even knowing it, Tommy picked up the emotions contained in a news report or your own reactions while watching it.

- Chronic stomachaches, headaches, or other physical symptoms. Whereas cholic is common for infants, we are talking about older children here. Food allergies may also play a part for highly sensitive children. Juvenile migraines are also common for young empaths, although few children are diagnosed as early as I was at eight years old.

- Unexplained bad dreams or night terrors. These children often receive energetic information even while they sleep. This can translate to many a restless night for the child . . . and the rest of the family.

- Stress related to events that are age inappropriate. For example, does your seven-year-old worry entirely too much about events in the Middle East? Have you noticed that your child is painfully aware of the homeless crisis, animal abuse, racism, or other hot-button topics that are just way too big for a child so young?

These signs are usually the outward reflection of the inner turmoil that these children are experiencing as a result of feeling as if they were drowning in the world's emotions. There are also some very specific personality traits that are usually seen within these children as well.

- The Protector – They are protective of siblings and even their parents. These children would literally throw themselves in front of a bus to protect their families and friends. Maybe your toddler is the first to jump and run when the baby cries? Or perhaps Kim is the one who always seems to make friends with the outcast. This is because they are so highly aware of the pain of others, they would do anything to prevent it.

- The Little Mamma – Do you find that your child is often trying to parent you? Do they try to take care of the whole family? This is the small child who offers you her blankie because she just KNOWS you feel bad. She is the one who parents her dolls in a very intuitive fashion. While most children will feed their dolls or put them to bed, your Little Mama will take this to extremes— even suffering what looks like empty nest syndrome if they are separated from the focus of their maternal instincts. These behaviors can also be seen in boys, though it's not as common.

- The Fixer – This child wants to take care of everything before problems manifest. This is a different form of The Protector but may present in some children, and especially boys, as the need to fix everything or everyone around them. This child is more likely to be the one making goofy faces to distract his parents before they start fighting. If this fails, he may also resort to disruptive or unacceptable behavior, or perhaps may even begin to become physically ill in a subconscious attempt to distract his parents and diffuse the situation.

- The Copy Cat – This empath child will often mirror the most dominant personality in their space. For parents of these children, it can be like living with Dr. Jekyl and Mr. Hyde. One minute your child is playing happily on the playground with her friends; then some new children show up, and all of a sudden, your sweet and loving little girl who loves to share has been replaced by a squealing hellion who is now ripping someone's ball from their hands with a resounding, "MINE!" This is because they will pick up the energy from their friends, and it simply takes children longer to disconnect. These children are stuck in a perpetual game of emotional "monkey see, monkey do."

- The Human Lie Detector – This child instinctively knows when you are being untruthful and does not handle deception well. Even if they don't know how to say they don't believe you, they are exceptionally talented at letting you know they no longer trust you. It is hard to rebuild that trust with these children because, with them, it is ALWAYS personal. Sometimes these children will seem highly distrusting of strangers until they shock you one day by striking up a conversation with a random person as if they were old friends.

## How Do I Raise My Empath Child?

If you read that list and found yourself nodding along, chances are your child is an empath. Congratulations! You have been given one of the most special and challenging gifts a parent could ever ask for in a child. Most likely, they have already both amazed you and tried you to your limit—probably even in the same day! These children are incredibly bright and talented souls, but they can feel overwhelmed and intimidated by the energy overload we all know so well.

Validate their feelings and emotions! This is the most important thing you can do as a parent for your empathic child, whether your child is nine months, nineteen, or ninety-nine. Teach them that what they are experiencing is real, and that it is alright that they feel the way they do in the moment. The second next important thing you can do for them is to teach them to recognize the patterns within their own lives. Let them know the difference between their OWN emotions and those of the people around them. As the parent of a highly sensitive or gifted child, you will have the challenging task of teaching them to navigate through a world that is full of intense emotions, positive and painful alike. You can help them learn to trust their own bodies by allowing them to give voice to what they are thinking and feeling. Allowing them to express this helps them understand what's going on within their systems.

There are many things that we as parents of these great kids can do to help them navigate the vast world of feelings and emotions that is there to meet them every day.

First and foremost, CHECK YOURSELF. There is a good chance that if your very young child is suddenly moody or throwing a tantrum, it's because they are picking up on your emotions, and they don't know how to express what they are feeling. It is also important to take a moment to shield yourself if you know you are having an especially stressful day, BEFORE you step into your child's space. Oftentimes when our child is unhappy, we as parents become uneasy, frustrated, or even panicky. If you have a young child that is sick or especially fitful on a particular day, remember it is okay to step away to regain your composure. In the case of an empath child, it's not only acceptable, but it's also recommended because your angst will only make their symptoms worse.

## Exercises for Children

### Flour and Water

Teach your child what's happening in their bodies when they are feeling angry or unhappy. At around the developmental age of four, children will begin to understand visual metaphors. You can give your child a clear cup with some water in it and let them see how clear the water is. Add a couple of teaspoons of flour to the water and stir it up. "See how the water's all foggy and you can't see clearly anymore? This is what it's like in your brain when you are angry or scared. Everything is blurry, and it's hard to think clearly. But if you just wait a few moments . . ." By then the flour should begin to settle to the bottom of the glass and the water will slowly become clear again. "Then all the feelings settle back down like this flour, and you can see clearly again!" This is a good way to transition a child slowly back from the edge of a meltdown, IF you see it coming.

**What's Mine?**

Help them learn the difference between their own emotions and those of the people around them. Now that they have a grip on WHAT they are feeling, encourage them to discern if this energy is even theirs at all. This can be very confusing for a young child who, by nature, is "ME" oriented. To a child, everything is about them because they haven't developed their awareness of the world. You can help them with this by asking them how they feel while in a room with other people. If they have a very strong connection with someone in particular, have them spend some time alone with that person.

First, ask them how they are feeling while they are interacting with the people or person. Then have them spend a few quiet minutes alone doing some belly breathing or doing something quiet that they enjoy— something like playing with blocks or drawing a picture. Then ask them again how they are feeling. This will help them start to understand that not everything they are experiencing is theirs. You can then help them redirect their own energy when they recognize other people's emotions, and work out how to process them correctly.

**Give Your Child "The Bucket"**[2]

A simple sand pail will do just fine for this analogy. Explain to your child that everything that happens throughout the day will "fill up her bucket":

the people she meets, interactions at school, feelings that she may pick up, and so on. The more that happens during the day, the faster her bucket will fill. When it is full, emotions will start spilling out. By pointing out to your child that maybe their bucket is getting too full and suggesting that they take some quiet time to work on emptying it, you are validating their feelings and giving them the room to work out what belongs in there or not. There are many tools you can share with your child to help them empty their emotional bucket again. However, it's vital that you let them empty it for themselves and not take it from them or try to fix what spills out. This technique works so well for children that often empath parents decide to pick up a bucket for themselves. If you are feeling overwhelmed or stressed, maybe your own bucket is full. When you mention this to your children, they will instinctively understand that maybe mom needs some extra quiet time, because they know only too well what an overloaded bucket feels like.

## Belly Breathing

As we mentioned in the breath work section, healthy breathing patterns are essential to a healthy, energetic body. You can explain even to small children how to recognize when their breath is becoming shallow and fast. Tell them that this type of breathing can actually make the things they are feeling feel worse; then teach them to do belly breathing with their whole tummy. Show them how, when they take a deep breath in, their belly comes out, and when they exhale, it relaxes again. Once they see how to take the deep breath, start tapping rhythmically about once a second. Now you can help them count the taps as they breathe. Inhale for 4 taps, hold for 2, exhale for 4, (with older kids, you can hold here for 2) and repeat this pattern for five to ten breaths. These counts can always be adjusted according to your own child's individual needs. For younger children, you can begin to teach them to control their breath by teaching them to blow bubbles with a wand available at any dollar store, and for indoor use, you can put some bubble solution into a shallow cake dish and have them blow the biggest one they can. This requires them to breathe slowly and steadily, or the bubble will burst.

## Meditation for Children

There are many techniques available on the Internet to help your child meditate.[3] Make sure they are comfortable with the belly breathing above, before moving on to meditation exercises. However, do not expect them to sit still longer than one minute for each year of their developmental age, at the most.

## Emotion Flashcards

When your child is feeling overwhelmed, it can be hard for them to understand, much less express, what is going on within their tiny systems. It can be helpful to give them some visual cues to help them to get a grip on what's happening to them, and why. You can make the cards for yourself with clip art, pictures from magazines, and books, or you can help your child draw their own pictures. For example, you might ask, "Can you draw a mad face?" (Then show them what a mad face looks like). You can also use pictures of your child and the family making a sad face, happy face, sleep face, etc. There are also several sources online that offer free printable flash cards for this purpose.[4]

For very young children (ages two to three, developmentally) you can show them the card and name the emotions. You can line up a few and ask them, "Jasmine, can you point to confused?" Or you can pick a card and ask them to copy the face. For slightly older children (ages four to six, developmentally), you can then take it a step beyond just labeling emotions to understanding that these emotions are caused by something. You can add a second set of cards to the games and start talking about the reasons behind these emotions. You can also skip the extra cards and just say the causes, but they miss out on many visual cues this way. You can make these cards based on your own child's individual personality, needs, and motivations.

Think about what causes your child to become overwhelmed? What calms them down? What are they passionate about (both love and hate)? What scares them? Makes them happiest? Use these things to create imaginary situations, events, or anything else that may apply to them. Let's call these the *cause cards*. Now you can have your child choose a cause card and match it to the appropriate emotion, or reversely, they can try to pick out all of the causes that might trigger that emotion.

At around the ages of six and up, developmentally, you can also begin to show them what to do when they match an emotion to the cause. For example, if the cause card says, "Going to the doctor," then your child can then choose the emotions they feel should match this: scared, sad, or maybe they don't mind so much. Once they have made this connection, you can then start to help them understand the connection between what is happening and how they feel. You can also start to talk to them about how to handle what they are feeling in those situations. Use the cards to tell stories. For example, Jimmy feels [*emotion*] because [*cause*] so he should try [*action*] and then he might feel [*emotion*]. Let them play with mixing and matching the situations and emotions, to find ways for calming down again.

## Other Abilities of Empath Children[5]

Marcie was three years old when her father was deployed to the Middle East. He had been gone for less than a month on a two-year deployment, when she woke up one morning cheerily saying, "Daddy's coming home!" Obviously, her mother brushed this off to the imagination of a child, but Marcie insisted again, "Daddy's coming home!" That same evening, Marcie's mother received a phone call that her brother-in-law had been killed in a car wreck. By the next morning, Marcie and her mother were on the way to the airport to pick up her dad for his brother's funeral. A few years later, when she was six years old, Marcie stunned her family once more with her unmistakable knowings when they were on a routine visit to the hospital. As they were walking inside, she pointed to an ambulance and said, "Macky's in that truck, and he's all burned up" as she burst into tears. Her mother tried to reassure her that her favorite uncle was not there at the hospital and that he was at work as usual. She pointed to the ambulance as it was opening to show Marcie that it wasn't her uncle Macky, but lo and behold, it actually was him. Apparently he had been burned in a gasoline fire while working in his mechanic's shop and had third-degree burns covering much of his upper body.

Marcie didn't know how to explain to her family how she knew these things. After the first couple of times, they began to see that Marcie had a talent that was rare indeed and began to pay more attention to her when she stated with confidence that something was about to take place.

What other, non-empath abilities do your children have? Do they talk to invisible people, do they describe deceased relatives, do they predict future events? These children will often sense things that others are unaware of. This may come in the form of them knowing that something isn't right with someone, so if Jillian comes crying to you about Grandma and this is unusual for her, she may not know how to express what she is experiencing.

Does your child take turns playing games with their imaginary friends? What if they were real? If little Jillian comes to you and tells you about her new invisible friend, and she begins to give you a detailed history of George's life, isn't it at least worth considering that perhaps she is gifted with more than just an active imagination?

Trevor would say, "If 'other dimensional beings' did exist, who would be more likely to see them and talk to them, children or adults? Could we be programming most our children out of talents today that, in a few more generations, may be considered to be commonplace? Remember, the greater the emotional sensitivity, the greater the challenge trying to operate in mainstream society."

## Resources

1. *Parenting an Empathic Child: Tips for Recognizing and Coping with an Empathic Child* by Jennifer Soldner
2. "The Bucket": http://www.bonbonbreak.com/helping-my-highly-sensitive-child/
3. See the Butterfly Meditation for children on http://www.OMGIcanmeditate.com (https://app.omgmeditate.com/#/kids-meditations/7/5)
4. Emotion flashcards:
   - http://bogglesworldesl.com/emotions_flashcards.htm
   - http://www.mes-english.com/flashcards/feelings.php
5. "Exploring the Social and Emotional Aspects of Gifted Children" by Deirdre V. Lovecky. Reprinted at http://sengifted.org/ with permission from Roeper Review.

# CHAPTER 19

# Mental Health and the Empath

By Trevor

> *A question that sometimes drives me*
> *hazy: am I or are the others crazy?*
> —ALBERT EINSTEIN

This book is not about mental health counseling. If you are in danger of harming yourself or others, please contact your local emergency services immediately.

Many empaths experience mental health challenges along the road to becoming thriving empaths. Being an empath means having the ability to experience the feelings, thoughts, or attitudes of other people. Confused empaths mistake them as their own. When we believe those feelings to be of our own creation, we try to fix them. Failure! Guaranteed! This brings us to the first set of challenges.

The Western world often discourages sensitivity and usually has a major distrust of anything that cannot be seen, touched, or scientifically measured. So when an empath reaches out for support from non-empaths, they risk being invalidated by their family, ill-considered friends, and especially, authority figures. Fortunately, in a world that is connected by the Internet, it is easier than ever to find experienced empaths who can provide help for the confused empath.

A major purpose of this book is to provide the exercises to help struggling empaths function in mainstream society. There are many close links between spiritual growth and mental health. Of all the processes provided here, the grounding techniques especially will help counteract any mental imbalance. However, there may be times when all these exercises seem insufficient.

The society we are living in is out of balance. Humanity is capable of feeding everybody but doesn't. More is spent on weapons than on education, and there is an enormous imbalance of wealth distribution. To most empaths, who appreciate just how much we are all connected, these are not descriptions of a healthy society. It is no wonder that we are often disoriented when growing spiritually at the same time that we are trying to keep rapport with the mainstream and "be one of them" in a dysfunctional world.

However, just having a human body could be described as a disorienting experience in itself. It was the French philosopher Pierre Teilhard de Chardin who said, "We are not human beings having a spiritual experience. We are spiritual beings having a human experience." If we are to accept that perspective, then it becomes a short step to the thought that someone who is particularly sensitive to the spiritual dimensions of life could easily be overwhelmed by the dense and heavy vibrations of taking on a human body. Indigenous cultures recognize the potential for shamans and healers in what Western culture calls mental illness.[1] We have lost what it means to walk in those worlds and be initiated into their mysteries. When society denies psychic abilities and the very existence of spirit, it condemns those people with labels of delusion and insanity.

If you are having difficulty living day-to-day, please contact a licensed health care professional.[2] There are a few practitioners in Western healthcare who understand what it means to be an empath. There are many more who list themselves as skilled with working with highly sensitive people (HSPs), and this can be a good category of professional to look for. Using pharmaceuticals is not ideal; they are neither a cure nor a long-term solution. As a short-term Band-Aid, however, prescription drugs can provide assistance for moving from being unable to get through the day to being able to regain a foothold in what most of the world calls reality. Seriously! We still believe that if it's a choice between not being able to function in the world and getting whatever help is available, it is better to get what help is available until we are able to function well enough to find better help.

Yet again (alright, we know it's the third time!), remember, the greater the emotional sensitivity, the greater the challenge trying to operate in mainstream society.

## Resources

1. "How a West African Shaman Helped My Schizophrenic Son in a Way Western Medicine Couldn't" by Dick Russell in the *Washington Post*, March 24, 2015
2. National Alliance for the Mentally Ill: http://www.nami.org
   (Please note that this is mainstream resource and the people here are unlikely to have any special understanding if you start talking about being an empath.)

# CHAPTER 20

# Thriving as Healers in a Changing World

By Trevor

> *If you feel like you don't fit in, in this world, it is*
> *because you are here to help create a new one.*
> —JOCELYN DAHER

When I started my daily practice of meditation back in 1975, it was something for pop stars and eccentrics. Today, meditation and mindfulness are accepted in the mainstream—you can see it practiced from boardrooms to prisons, from schools to living rooms throughout the world. Society is changing so fast that the idea of empaths experiencing others' emotions regardless of physical proximity is shifting out of science fiction and into daily reality.

An ideal skill as an empath is being able to return to a childlike state, where emotions flow effortlessly. I say *ideal* with the knowledge that there are few, even among thriving empaths, who can easily allow others' emotions to routinely pass through them. For the confused empath, those very emotions can be mistaken by society for a mental health crisis because that is the limit of mainstream understanding, and there are certainly no scientific measures to identify us. As we better learn how to process other people's emotions, we become centered and balanced. In turn, this is self-enhancing, as that stability allows us to become more skillful empaths.

So what do I mean by "thriving as healers"?

Let's get the semantics out of the way, starting off with the difference between healing and curing.

With curing, there is a symptom, a disease, to be removed; however, during this process, the patient does not change. Often, if a symptom is removed without intrinsic healing, different issues will occur until the underlying energetic cause is resolved. When we receive healing, we change as does our relationship to the illness, as we understand what our body had been trying to tell us.

Secondly, the concept that anyone heals another is false. There are only people who help others heal themselves. In fact, there are no *healers* only *facilitators of healing*. That said, if we can agree that the word *healer* really means a *facilitator of healing*, it is easier to use one word rather than three.

The Light Projector exercise in the chapter "Shielding" is about sending out energy instead of taking in others' emotions. This is a healing process. Picking up the energy of others is like a doorbell. Someone is letting us know that they are there, most often because they are in need of help. Sending light and love is answering that call. For thriving empaths, being healers doesn't mean that we all have to be massage therapists, acupuncturists, or life coaches, although that may be appropriate for some of you. Primarily, healing is about becoming channels for sending energy to people in need. Seperately, there is also a strong aspect of healing in finding our soul purpose.

It doesn't matter whether we are a school teacher or a construction worker. Developing and using our natural talents keeps the energetic flow moving, and as a result, we feel better within ourselves. By aligning with our soul purpose, we raise the level of passion and awareness in the world around us. When we are off purpose, our energy is drained. When we are on purpose, our energy flows, and we help heal our planet. Finding our soul purpose is one of the most significant steps we can take toward healing ourselves.

Where do your gifts lie? What has to happen for you to start using them, or pick up using them from where you may have left off? (Hint: find yourself a coach if you feel challenged answering those questions.)

The more we move in the right direction, the more the Universe will support us by showing us the next, and only the next, step to take. There have been times when I have asked for some idea of what follows, only to be gently reminded, "One step at a time." We look for patterns and certainty to remain within our comfort zones when we ask, "Okay, now I know what I am supposed to be doing today; what am I going to be doing next week, next month, next year?" We are rarely given those insights. Primarily, most of our questions are best answered by remaining in the present moment. Also, there is a sequence to learning, just as a child starting multiplication doesn't need to know about algebra and the first-grade reader doesn't need to comprehend Shakespeare.

And yet, just as I was getting used to the idea that I was only going to be given one step at a time, a sense of my own soul purpose started to form. The concept is of an Academy of Lightworkers on the same scale as today's universities and hospitals. When someone goes into the hospital, it is rarely for a particular doctor, but rather for the whole support team. Today, most holistic healers are working as solo entrepreneurs. The vision is that at some time in the future, the client would be able to receive treatment from a healing center made up of hundreds of practitioners. This academy would also serve as a school where people can learn the energetic arts from multiple teachers. Of course, in the bigger scheme of things, the Academy of Lightworkers will, I am sure, be just one of many such centers around the world.

The inspiration for writing this book was twofold: First, I wanted other confused empaths to learn from my own struggles and to be able to use these abilities without being overwhelmed by them. Second, my vision of a healthy world is one with as many thriving empaths as possible.

The instruction to treat your neighbor as yourself is not needed for an empath. We know that the conventional concept of individuality is vastly overrated. When we feel the pain of the world around us, we understand that we cannot hurt another without hurting ourselves. In a world of empaths, crime, inequality, injustice, and wars cannot exist.

Many of us grew up feeling different, misunderstood, isolated, and often, outcast. That is no longer necessary. We are changing as we connect with each other, and in the process, the world around us is also changing. When we consider the possibility that we are evolving into "*homo-empathicsus*," then we can see empaths as potential forerunners of world peace.

# CHAPTER 21

# Acknowledgements

## Trevor's Acknowledgements

In somewhat chronological order:

- My parents, Naomi and Philip, and my sister, Caroline. Yes, I picked you for good reason; I knew that even on those days when I thought, "What was I thinking at the time?"
- Maharishi Mahesh Yogi and Transcendental Meditation (www. TM.org) for bringing into the world the meditation technique that put me on this path.
- Allen Schoer, Twila Thompson, Gifford Booth of TAI Partners (www. thetaigroup.com) for the creativity that I used to call zen, and the art of acting.
- Donald Epstein of Wise World Seminars (www.wiseworldseminars. com) for the Network Spinal Analysis entrainments and Twelve Stages of Healing breath work.
- Sri Sri Ravi Shankar of the Art of Living Foundation (www.artofliving. org) for the breath work and the shaktipat.
- Joy Perkins for moving beyond first impressions, and Kelly Hewitt for the spoonful of soup.

- Jan Marszalek of NLP Learning Systems (www.nlplearningsystems. com) for the tool chest full of techniques taught with love, wisdom, and generosity.
- Danica Hershberger for being there for almost every step of my conscious journey as an empath.
- Bonnie Cook Yardley for introducing me to the Akashic records and instructing me to disavow my promise of "Never again!"
- Chris Largent of The Seventh Academy (www.theseventhacademy. org) for expanding my concepts of Plato, history, philosophy, astrology, and more besides.
- The Allies and their dragonfly. This book is just one of your gifts.
- Emma Churchman (www.emmachurchman.com) for the soul purpose coaching that opened the first page of this chapter of my life.
- My vibe tribe community in Asheville, North Carolina—you know who you are!
- JJ, with love, for such unexpected and knowledgeable assistance.
- And my wife and children, Lisa Lewis, Ethan, and Sarah for finding, opening, and then filling my heart.

## Abbigayle's Acknowledgements

- My sister and lifelong partner in crime, Valerie. Thank you for always being my motivation. I am a better person because I always knew you were watching.
- My vibe tribe. David, for always being my sounding board. Jeff, for never giving up on me, even when I deserved it. Horace, for being my teacher, coach, and somewhat mismatched friend.
- My pow-wow family. Bear Hug, Pony, and especially Chipa Wolfe for creating a space for me (and everyone) to learn about my heritage and for allowing me to be a part of the tribe.

- All of my mentors and teachers who have pushed me to live up to my potential and never let me settle for "good enough." Special thanks to Coach Matthew Hill, Kady Hall, and Grace Price for going above and beyond to be a light in my world when it was cloaked in darkness.
- Last but not least, my twin flame and life partner, Dennis, for giving me the courage to hope again. My reason is you.

# CHAPTER 22

# About The Authors

## Trevor Lewis

Trevor was born a mystic. He started his twice daily meditation practice in 1976, at age twenty, and has actively used multiple personal transformation technologies ever since. These include Neuro-Linguistic Programming (NLP), breath work, and his own form of Emotion Clearing, among many others. His many teachers have been a mixture of Eastern and Western, including some of the best teachers NOT on the planet, who have
been giving him some pretty clear instructions to follow in recent years. He gave up a thirty-seven-year career in Information Technology in 2015 to move into fulfilling his true purpose in this life. His overriding passion is raising consciousness, and he is now emphasizing his role of teacher, coach, and speaker for the empath community, helping people move from being confused empaths to thriving empaths!

He moved from his native England to America in 1988 and now lives in Asheville, North Carolina, with his wife, Lisa, and their two children.

You can email him at Trevor@ThrivingEmpath.com.

## Abbigayle McKinney

When Abbey was six years old, her mother became pregnant with her little sister. At the time, she was living almost sixteen miles away with her grandparents. She would wake in the mornings with horrible nausea and developed an acute sensitivity to smells for nearly two months. Then, just as suddenly as it came, it was gone. Her life-long empath abilities had shown up in the form of her mother's morning sickness.

As a child, she used to spend all of her free time alone in the woods talking to the trees and the plants and learning from her guides how to listen to the energy of everything around her. She had the opportunity to study the native plant medicine of the North Georgia Mountains with a traditional Cherokee medicine man and followed up many years later by becoming certified as a shaman in the Peruvian tradition. She uses crystals, herbs, energy, sound, channeling, and reading the Akashic records to offer a flexible, balanced, and well-rounded approach to healing her clients.

She uses her gifts and personal experience to help guide, teach, and heal the collective old souls trapped in teenage bodies that she seems to attract like a magnet. She also volunteers her services as a crisis counselor for people with mental illness.

You can email her at AbbeyMcKinney1083@gmail.com.

Made in the USA
Middletown, DE
09 June 2022

66922655R00116